FORGIVENESS—
A KEY TO SUCCESS

Bill Krause

All scripture references are quoted from the
New King James Version of the Holy Bible
unless otherwise noted.

ISBN #0-9678277-0-X

Write:
Kingsway Publishing
P.O. Box 904
North Highlands, CA 95660

916-334-6700

CONTENTS

FOREWORD

HOW TO GET UNSTUCK AND MOVE ON

Have you been in that place where you wanted to go forward and didn't know how to get started? You wanted to do something positive with your life, but your life wouldn't seem to take that direction.

What keeps us from doing what we want to do, from going where we want to go?

Taking an offense and becoming bitter with someone has the ability to stop us in our tracks. It is a hidden trap that bogs us down in the mire. We become immovable, immobile, and debilitated by our own unwillingness to forgive, forget and move on. Success comes from forgiveness.

INTRODUCTION

I have always been intrigued by people who have done the impossible, so to speak. The Wright Brothers, Thomas Edison, Roger Bannister, who broke the four-minute mile in 1954, Eric Liddle who ran for Great Britain in the 1924 Olympics, Pete Maravich known as "Pistol Pete" who had a dream to become one of basketballs greatest legends, and in fact, became the youngest inductee into the Basketball Hall of Fame. And, another favorite is Chuck Yeager who broke the sound barrier in 1947.

In the lives of these people there were limitations set by others or circumstances. There were obstacles to overcome, yet the desire to succeed was greater than any fear, risk, intimidation or insecurity. They achieved what some people would have thought was impossible.

As you read the following accounts of people with everyday varying circumstances—barriers of resentment and hurt that tried to stifle their lives—you will see how forgiveness brought them to a place of removing those barriers. Forgiveness can do the impossible by removing long-term hurts or resentments.

I believe as you read this book you will learn:

- What barriers the lack of forgiveness brings

- The results of forgiveness

- And, the freedom forgiveness brings to the lives of those who choose to forgive.

As the author's wife, I pray as you read about the individuals in this book and you see how their barriers of unforgiveness were broken, how their lives were changed, and the course of their future altered for the good, you too will will begin to break the barriers in your life and experience the joy, peace, freedom, and success that forgiveness brings.

Mrs. Cindy Krause

CHAPTER ONE
FREE TO BE YOU

As we go along through life, many of us struggle for our independence. We want to be an individual. We want to be unique, able to stand alone.

When we walk in forgiveness, we are able to do that. We can make our own decisions, do what we want to do, and be what we want to be.

When we walk in unforgiveness, our life is determined by others. We are no longer able to do certain things, to go to the places we want to go, or to have the relationships that we truly need.

When Carol, Barb, and Rich were growing up, they were typical brother and sisters. They had their times of joy and their times of disagreement. Their father died when they were in their teen years. Rich, being the oldest, began to help support the family and shoulder the responsibility. While finishing high school, Barb and Carol helped keep the house clean and meals on the table while Mom went off to work. All went well, considering the challenges they faced.

One day after Carol, the youngest, graduated, they were all at home for a family dinner. Before they knew it, they were in the middle of a family argument. Carol felt that it was all her fault because the argument was started by her. How could she do this to her family? How could they ever forgive her? That night Carol left home, the people whom she loved and needed, those who had always stood by her were no longer part of her life.

Carol had severed her family ties and made herself a part of a lonely world where people did not care about her and didn't recognize her value. At Christmas time she was not with her family. On her mother's birthday she could not give Mom a card or present. There were no more of those wonderful lunches with her sister, no more opportunities with her older brother to get the advice she needed.

Carol was no longer free to make her own choices, no longer free to do what she wanted to do or to go where she wanted to go. She could not pick up the phone and tell her mom she loved her—all because of unforgiveness. In this case, she would not forgive herself, and now she locked herself in prison because of it.

Fifteen years later Carol was reunited with Barb and Rich. She discovered that they had never been mad at her. It was all a big misunderstanding. Barb and Rich had searched diligently to find her over the years. They longed to have her be a part of their life, but Carol was nowhere to be found.

One of the most unfortunate parts is that Carol's mother passed away two years before their reunion. Carol wept deeply when she found out about her mother. She had missed so much, so many very important events, all because she was locked in prison, a prison she had built herself. She was the warden, the cell guard, and the parole commission. She remained in that prison, unable to do what she wanted to do until she humbled herself, returned to her family, and accepted their forgiveness.

So many of us have a similar story. We have locked ourselves into a prison because of unforgiveness. We are no longer free. We are unable to freely go to the places we used to enjoy.

Another group of prisoners bound by their unforgiveness thinks that their bars are good for them, that the bars protect them from the dark, cruel world. They believe they will not be hurt again if they just stay behind the bars. This is a great theory, but it cannot work. Our freedom is stripped from us. The same bars that protect us from being hurt keep us from being healed. The hurt put us into prison, and only love will set us free and make us whole.

Let's look at Becky's story. Becky, at a young age, found the right man, or so she thought. She was married and began to live the adult life. Out of her parent's house, she was now able to do what she wanted. Her parents had been strict; now she was out of that prison. It was not long before she found herself in greater pain. Her husband was abusive. Her marriage had turned into a war that she was not sure she could survive.

After two years she built up the courage and got a divorce, swore off marriage, vowing to stay free. Five years passed, and she met another wonderful man to marry. Her pain had been buried deep enough to forget, but unfortunately not removed. Loneliness won out over pain. The wounds were not healed, though covered over enough to forget. She was able to receive parole from her prison for a brief time. Like most prisoners, she found herself back in prison. Marriage number two was a bust. More pain, more misery, and back to prison for another seven years.

Now she made a new vow, "I am putting myself back into prison. No human visitors will be allowed. This time I will build the bars twice as thick so no human can get in. I have the solution to loneliness. I will take in stray dogs and keep them in prison with me. Since no one wants us anyway, we will be safe and take care of each other."

It was a nice plan but unreal. I also have a dog. He is a wonderful asset to our family and fun to be around, but no replacement for wife, children, or friends. Remember what God said in the garden while Adam was surrounded by all the wonderful animals that he had named. The Lord God said, "It is not good that man should be alone. I will make him a helper comparable to him." (Genesis 2:18.) Pets are great, but people need people.

Well, the good news is that Becky has been paroled from prison again. This time it is for good with a full pardon. Yes she has been rehabilitated. The wounds have been completely healed. The bars that kept her from being hurt, and also from being loved, are all taken down and destroyed. Becky is walking in forgiveness. She has people who love her, and she is able to love them.

It is so wonderful to see Becky loving people and helping to set others free. In prison she was unable to help people, to reach through the bars. Now that she is free she has a mission and a purpose. Becky is able to help others. She now understands where they have been, as well as how to set them free. (No cause to worry about the dogs. Now that Becky is set free, they receive more attention than ever from her and her new friends.)

We all want to be free. It's no fun being in prison. At times it can seem safe, but there is so much we have to give up to obtain that safety. The safety of prison is not real because all the while we are dying on the inside, wilting away to nothing. We are unable to fulfill our call and divine destiny. Prison has its benefits and can even be used to make someone other than the prisoner suffer. The truth is the prisoner is the one who loses the most rights and gives up the greatest benefits. The prisoner loses the most freedom and pays the biggest price.

Midge's story will help to cement this point. Midge was a woman full of life, a loving wife and an active mom involved with her children. Her husband, Ted, was in the insurance business. As the years went by, the business grew, and he was able to provide a comfortable living for his family.

As has happened all too often, Ted got involved with his secretary at work. The relationship progressed for some time, then Midge found out. She was devastated. Her world had fallen apart. She could not find it in her heart to forgive her husband or the other woman. (Now we can all agree that this was devastating news, that this would crush even the best of us. What would we do? How would we react? Could we survive?)

As you can imagine, Midge's life was devastated. She became very bitter and refused to forgive her husband or the other woman. Midge placed herself in solitary confinement. Deep in the bowels of prison, she could no longer be a mom to her kids. Her bitterness kept her from loving her kids, from being there when they needed her. Her friends lost her. There were no more times of coffee and chatting, no more lunches or trips to the mall, and no more talks about how to raise kids.

She ended up moving back in with her mom. Because of the deep confinement of her prison caused by her unforgiveness, she was unable to celebrate Christmas, sing a birthday song, or enjoy a Thanksgiving dinner.

The truth is that this would be a difficult situation for anyone to be in.

Midge ended up with cancer racing through her body. It is true that many people suffered loss as a result of Midge's imprisonment. It was, however, Midge who suffered the greatest loss. She lost everything that she held dear.

She was never able to love again as a result of her unforgiveness. Her husband was gone, and I suppose we can understand that. She also lost her kids, her friends, her mom, and her life. She died of cancer. As she lay there in that bed at 68 pounds, unable to speak, she asked for a writing board. Before her last dying breath she wrote a derogatory remark about her ex-husband. What a miserable way to live. What a miserable way to die.

There is no excuse for Ted's action. He was one hundred percent wrong. But being wronged does not give us the right to judge others and destroy our lives. The very best way to get even is to receive the grace, rise above the situation, and forgive. Then we can be released from prison so that we are free to live life and free to help others. No matter how much we make anyone suffer, we suffer more. No matter what price anyone else pays, the one who does not forgive pays a higher price.

Isn't it true that we all want to be who we really are?

We want to succeed and have a life worth enjoying.

To be truly free and to stay out of our self-imposed prison, we must choose to walk in forgiveness. It is a choice, a choice that only we can make. Offenses will come. We are all given many opportunities to take up an offense. Although these offenses come to all, do not take them up! We can say, "But you don't understand." The truth is you don't understand the cost. We can say, "It's not our nature or personality to forgive." But we must choose to change and adjust so that we can avoid our self made prison. We can say, "You don't know what they did to me, how deep the hurt is!" Maybe not, but I know that if you don't forgive, you will put yourself in prison, and many other people whom you deeply love will be hurt as a result of your imprisonment. Their pain will cause you even more pain.

You need to choose forgiveness so you are free to be who you really are, to go where you want to go, and to stay out of prison. This is your ticket for parole. The greatest advantage of forgiveness is your freedom.

CHAPTER TWO
WHAT'S YOUR CHOICE?

Tim was a great kid. He grew up in a middle class family with his brothers and sisters. He had a loving dad and mom. At 16, Tim was well liked and popular in school. He achieved good grades, was a leader in his class and was involved in many activities.

One day Tim and three of his buddies pulled a boyhood stunt. They obtained some beer, drank more than their share, and began to get silly. They came up with the bright idea to go over to their school and climb up the flagpole. After climbing to the top, they began to sing, cause a ruckus, and make a major scene. When the folks in charge heard the commotion, the boys fled before they could be caught. The next day at school everyone became aware of the situation but did not know who was involved.

It was announced that the weekend dance would not go on if the culprits were not discovered. Of the four, Tim was a young man of integrity. He went to the school authorities and confessed his part. After all, it was the right thing to do and others should not have to suffer for his actions. They wanted to know who else was involved, but Tim would not disclose anything but his part. He was the only one who came forward, and the school officials decided to make an example of him in front of the faculty, students, and their families. Tim's friends were not willing to admit to their part, and he was deeply wounded by their betrayal. Tim was also embarrassed that everyone knew what he had done.

Tim's life drastically changed after that incident. He could not forget the weakness of his friends or the public embarrassment from the staff.

That summer things cooled off from the incident, but heated up on the inside of Tim. He dropped out of sports— he probably would have played pro had he not quit. He stopped being a part of school activities and immersed himself in his studies. The whole thrust and course of his life was changed. Tim had always been a leader, active in helping others, and someone to be counted on. He still appeared in many ways to be the same, however, something had happened to his fire; his competitive edge was gone.

Bob's story is very similar, yet things turned out so differently. In Bob's junior year at high school the principal called an all-school assembly. All the students, the principal, the teachers, and other dignitaries were gathered. Bob and four other fellows decided to fire off a cherry bomb firecracker. It was an exciting moment with a loud bang. Everyone was startled. The teachers did not know who did it. They continued with the assembly until Bob and the boys decided to do it again since it was so funny. Well the assembly ended abruptly and all the students were sent back to class. Immediately an announcement came over the PA system: School elections were cancelled until the culprits were found.

Bob thought it over. He then went to the principal and

asked what would happen to those who did it if they confessed. After being assured that the matter would not leave that office, Bob confessed but refused to tell on the others. He knew it was not his place to tell their story. No one else came forward. The principal told the staff. The student body found out, and Bob received a three-day suspension, as well as after-school time.

Bob, however, did not take offense but swallowed his pride and forgave the principal. He continued to participate in sports and except for occasional high school storytelling times, forgot the incident.

Tim went on in school and obtained a good education, met his wife, had children and obtained a great job. It all looked good on the exterior, but inside Tim had died. Unforgiveness for the high school leadership swelled in his heart. This stopped him from being bold in his convictions, unable to follow through with decisions, he rambled aimlessly unable to communicate his true feelings, the point of his communication lost in a sea of words.

As successful as he was in life, Tim was unfulfilled. He was not doing what he really wanted to do in life. Tim had stopped growing on the inside. A great man with great potential was stifled by doing a foolish stunt and then allowing himself to fall into unforgiveness.

For over 30 years Tim walked in unforgiveness. He held himself back, unable to reach the fullness of his potential. Because of an incident at age 16 he was unable to go beyond the lid that he had placed over his life. A young man with much ability and strong potential now all lying dormant. Some would say, "Oh he just didn't get the breaks; it had nothing to do with him." Wrong! It was his inability to walk in the most powerful force, called forgiveness.

Bob, like Tim, went on to marry his wonderful wife and had his beautiful children. The big difference was Bob was free in life. He had forgiven the high school officials and had not concerned himself with the buddies who did not come forward. The others who did not confess, by the way, all ended up with tragic lives: drugs, alcohol, divorce, failing in their jobs. One even committed suicide.

Bob continued on in life. He was elected captain of the track team, developed a successful career in the construction industry, and is now able to help and love people without reserve. Bob is confident in his decisions, continues to achieve his goals, and is a leader in his field.

Some of the benefits of forgiveness are to live a peaceful, successful life, to come to the fullness of our potential, and to be free to choose our path instead of it being determined by our past. We have so much to live for, so much we could do. If—and that is a big word—we will begin to let our unforgiveness be uncovered, lifted off of us and cast away, we will begin to obtain new heights.

Remember Tim? Well, after over 30 years he admitted he had unforgiveness for those folks. He forgave them, and his life has been on an accelerated pace ever since. He has grown and matured by the hour. The lid is off, and he has sprouted into a tall oak tree. His business has multiplied and prospered. He does in two months what he used to do in a year. His wife is more beautiful and radiant than ever (what we are does affect others). His children have begun to abound in every area. His dreams of many years are coming to pass. He is living in a whole new world. The vitality of his youth has been renewed. He has freed himself to reach the fullness of his potential. It appears he will go beyond being a tall oak tree and become a towering redwood, extending beyond the clouds.

Forgiveness is a choice. It is up to each of us to do it. We reap the greatest benefit or the greatest devastation. It is up to you; it is up to me.

The greatest benefit of forgiveness is to allow ourselves to go for the gold, to be all we can be, and to achieve great results for ourselves and for others.

Have you allowed yourself to be in Tim's old position? Have you allowed a blast from the past to destroy your dreams? Now is your opportunity to turn things around, to get back on track, and to be all you can be.

Just by forgiveness

Dennis I am so happy I forgave you 30 yrs ago. I remember those heavy heavy rolling balls rolling off my back, what a relief of true forgiveness

10-15-15

CHAPTER THREE
ABLE TO BE CREATIVE

They say today that we are what we eat. However, a greater truth is that we are what we think. The Bible tells us that even as a man thinks so is he. If we are what we think (and we are), then our thoughts should be wisely guided and greatly protected.

One of the great advantages of forgiveness is clear thinking. When we become bitter or hate someone, bitterness and hatred begin to consume our thoughts and direct our actions.

I gave a message some time ago called, "Temporary Insanity." It was a message explaining that when we become angry, we lose touch with reality, say things we don't mean, and do things we would not normally do. The trouble with anger is that we begin saying and doing things we don't mean or want to be part of our lives. If we don't get a handle on it, we start thinking about what we said and what we did, and it begins to become real to us.

If you will take an open look at your life, you will see that you think about things before you do them. You do not wake up one day and get a divorce; first you think on the negative over and over. After thinking on your marital problems, they become overwhelming and you end the relationship.

The scripture says to be angry and sin not. If we don't cast down every evil imagination and high thing that exalts itself against the will of God; if we don't stop ourselves from getting angry and saying the wrong things, they begin to consume us. We begin to act and think that way each day of our lives. We become steeped in our thinking, and before long a root of bitterness has entangled us. Wrong thoughts become a way of life. They stifle our creativity. It is easier to think negatively than positively. The trouble is that the results of these negative thoughts are not productive.

When we become bitter with someone, we start a process that makes us just like them. Remember, we are what we think. What happens to you when you get bitter with someone? You begin to think about what they said. You go over and over what they did. It consumes your thought life until you can recite and review it in your sleep. It is now a part of your life.

What have you been thinking on? The terrible thing that was done to you? In turn, you begin living out your thoughts, and the very thing that you have despised, you have become.

To help bring this alive, let me tell a story. I have a clear remembrance from when I was growing up of my dad coming home from work, sitting down in "his" chair, and reading the newspaper. Two words of good advice in our house were not to sit in Dad's chair and not to disturb him while he was reading the paper. I don't have any recollection of being bitter over this, but I thought on it often, and it had a great effect on my life.

When I was married and began to have my own family, I made sure I did not get hung up on the newspaper or have a designated chair that was for only my use. No, I wanted to be sure that I would never fall into that trap. I did like to read, so I was always ready to enjoy a good book. A special chair? Not me! What I did was move to the bedroom—that was my place of refuge. Don't disturb me if the door is closed. I am reading a good book, expanding my mind. No, not me, I was nothing like my dad. Instead of a chair, it was the bed. Instead of the newspaper, it was a good book. Different, yes, but exactly the same!

Remember when your mother told you in that crisp voice, "Shut that refrigerator door, you're letting the cold out." You swore up and down that when you had children, you would never do anything like that. You thought on it often, to guarantee to yourself that you would never say it. Now if you are willing to listen, you can hear yourselves saying to your children, "Shut that refrigerator door, you're letting the cold out."

We become like those with whom we are bitter. Why? Because we concentrate on it. Take an inventory of your life, and look at those things you said you didn't like and you would never do. I think you'll find them popping up all over the place. If you don't succeed in finding them yourself, it's all right. You might be a little prejudiced. Ask a friend to go over the list without a lot of your pre-explanation. Show them the list, and ask them if they see any of these areas in your life.

We become what we think. When our mind is free of unforgiveness, we are free to think creatively. In this busy world we live in today there are so many things that can steal our thoughts. There is very little time where the world today is quiet. There is a constant barrage of televisions in the restaurant, music in the mall, talk shows in the car. If there is silence, we start to look inside, and we can see what needs to be adjusted. When you add in any kind of unforgiveness, it is easy to become afraid of any quiet time. What if I begin to remember? Maybe I will have to forgive. How can I get even? When will it ever end?

With our minds racing and focusing on the negative, we shut down our creativity. We fail to recognize all the wonderful things that are around us or realize what could be around us. We begin to live our life in a box. We start closing down the passing lanes, and we find ourselves in a stall.

A great benefit of forgiveness is a mind that is free to think on things that are true, noble, just, pure, lovely, things of good report. If there is any virtue and if there is anything praiseworthy, think on these things.

It may be a good time for you to break out the old Walt Disney movie, *Pollyanna*. It is about a little girl who changed a whole town. That town was upside down and backward. It was full of bitterness, unforgiveness, selfishness, and hate. One little girl introducing "the glad game" was able to get people looking for something to be glad about instead of complaining all the time. She also quoted from Abraham Lincoln, "When you look for the good in mankind expecting to find it, you surely will." Two life-changing thoughts from one little girl. It's a movie with a simple truth that will bring about great results.

If you have read about any of the great people of this

nation, you know they were energetic, creative, and full of life. Most of them encountered great opposition and persecution. They maintained their creativity because they were able to stay focused and forgive those who came against them. They kept going against all odds. They knew their life would have more meaning if they would stay focused on solving the problem or creating the answer instead of being bogged down in unforgiveness.

What is your choice going to be? Are you going to drop the bitterness? Begin to forgive and forget. Allow your life to mean something in the positive instead of continuing in the negative.

Are you willing to break loose from the old pattern, to forgive, and to start the creative juices of your youth flowing again? Are you willing to forsake your future for the benefit of unforgiveness?

Do you remember that you are paying a greater price than anyone else? When you refuse to forgive, you bite off your nose to spite your face. Why continue to torture yourself and those around you? Make a commitment to yourself to press through this book. Begin to choose to forgive no matter what the cost, knowing that the benefit will far outweigh your efforts.

You are about to increase your value. Instead of being a bitter, unforgiving person, void of life, you will be a creative giant, solving problems and full of life.

Congratulations! If you have read this far, you want to be free. Turn the page to find out what forgiveness is.

CHAPTER FOUR
FORGIVENESS IS—

A Path to Freedom

The path we are to walk is one of forgiveness. Webster defines forgiveness as: The act of forgiving; the pardon of an offender, by which he is considered and treated as not guilty; to give up resentment against or the desire to punish.

> *"Enter by the narrow gate; for wide is the gate and broad is the way that leads to destruction, and there are many who go in by it.*
>
> *"Because narrow is the gate and difficult is the way which leads to life, and there are few who find it."*
>
> Matthew 7:13-14 (NKJ)

The narrow gate is forgiveness. There is only one choice and that is to forgive—with no exception, no deviation, no matter how wrong the other person is, and whatever the circumstance. This is truly a very narrow gate. You can see now why so few find it. It sounds and looks pretty much one way. That's because it is. Forgiveness should always come quickly, without reserve, no ifs or buts, just plain right now "I forgive you." That seems like small thinking, narrowmindedness. It is, but it is the road to freedom.

Here's Loyd's story of how the wide path became narrow. When Loyd was 12 years old, his mother got involved in a wrong relationship with another man. His parents remained married, though things were not settled. Loyd began to be involved with drugs, and it soon became a daily habit. Twenty-four years later Loyd's mother, after forty-four years of marriage to his father, requested a divorce so she could marry the man she had gotten involved with many years earlier. The pain that Loyd and his family experienced was beyond words, yet the pain and anguish he experienced because of his own bitterness far exceeded that of the actual event.

Loyd's relationship continued to be strained, to the point that his mother stormed out of a restaurant where they had met for breakfast. Their communication had fallen to an all-time low. This was used by Loyd to fuel his bitterness. His drug problem only got worse in spite of his continued and even stepped-up efforts to seek help.

Two and a half years ago Loyd returned to the narrow path. Even though he had become a Christian when he was young, bitterness had placed him on the broad path to destruction. That narrow path started again with a fresh commitment to Christ and an infilling of His Holy Spirit, which included an overdose of God's love.

Here's a quote from Loyd after walking in this narrow path for over two years:

Forgiveness is difficult at best and many times impossible without the power of God. The love of God in my life put me in position to have my eyes opened to my bitterness and disobedience to my mother and father. You see, I could hardly honor my mother when I was bitter with her. As the man of God placed in my life began to shepherd me and as God began to soften me, I was able not only to forgive my mother but to recognize her as a child of God.

Well, needless to say, things are much better for Loyd and his mother since he stepped onto the narrow path of forgiveness. There was no longer room for judgment or self-pity. Loyd had to take his end of the stick and deal with it. No excuses, no finger pointing, no blame shifting, just the narrow road of forgiveness.

Loyd can now minister to his mother in love. Her health is remarkably better. He is drug free, and there is peace in his home. Now he looks forward to each visit with Mom.

Let's take a closer look at that broad path that leads to destruction; the path that is much more often followed. You can see from Loyd's story that he came upon the broad path and stayed there for years. Highlights of some of the destruction: 25 years of daily drug use, which is enough destruction in itself. Loyd and his wife owned two businesses, and they had plenty of money coming in but always more going out. Their son was not going in the right direction. (How could he when the family was on the broad path?)

The broad path is so broad because there is always one more reason why we should not forgive. The hard thing about the human mind is that we can just keep expanding our reasons why. "I'm sorry" is not good enough. I have heard that before. The list of reasons to not forgive someone is long, and if for any reason we find out we don't have enough to keep the unforgiveness going, we create some new reasons.

Forgiveness is a choice. No rationale, explanation, psychology, excuse, reason, or judgment can make us forgive. We either choose the narrow path of forgiveness, the path that is difficult at the time but brings forth the fruit that is rich and sweet, or we choose the broad path, the one that is wide and easy. It brings temporary pain relief with only negative side effects.

Fred's story is different than Loyd's. Fred had been serving God for seven years. Delivered from alcohol, tragedy, and devastation, he and his wife, Sue, were living a very happy life with their five children. Fred had settled down and was working steadily. He was making good money, living in the best house they ever had, and driving nice vehicles. Life was real good.

Then one day Fred's boss cheated him out of his monthly bonus. Fred took it really hard. He quickly became disturbed and very angry with his boss. He had always worked hard, had done a good job, and did everything he could for his boss to succeed.

The day he found out, Fred happened to be with a couple of good friends who encouraged him to not take the offense, to roll it over onto the Lord. His friends reminded him that things were going well in his life, and it would all work out in his favor if he would forgive. As Fred left his two friends, he said, "That was all good advice all right, but I am going to get even with my boss."

Fred took the offense that day and began to travel the wide road of offense. He had all the reasons: I am a good employee, he promised me, I work hard for him, he lied to me, and so on, and so on. It all sounded good to Fred, and it did not take long for him to build his case. He was angry. He had been offended, and he would never let the boss forget it!

Just so you know right now, God warned Fred many times over the next year. God did everything imaginable to bring Fred out of his unforgiveness.

The path was broad, and there were so many reasons not to forgive his boss. There was, however, one good reason to get off the broad path: It leads to destruction. At the end of one year of unforgiveness, Fred lost his job, and his vehicles and his house had to be sold to pay debts. In one year he went from total victory to the loss of everything. Only his family; that was all he had left.

Is the wide path worth it? Can we afford the luxury of unforgiveness? In the path of unforgiveness anything goes, everything seems right. Have you ever walked that wide path? Have you ever used logic, justification, and reason to place yourself on that path of destruction? Oh, it feels so good at the time. We have thought it through, and we know we are right. After all, if they had done what was right, we would not be in this mess. You know that it is all their fault.

We go on and on until we are really committed to the wide path, the path that always leads to destruction. We need to realize that we always end up hurting ourselves more than the one we refuse to forgive. Oh yes, it hurts that one who is not forgiven. They lose you. The one who refuses to forgive loses everything. Is it worth it? Can we really afford it? Not at all!

The scripture tells us the wages of sin is death.

Unforgiveness is a sin. Worst of all, it separates us from God. When we are separated from God, we cannot get our best results. If we are going to receive a wage, for sure we want to receive a good wage. Forgiveness produces life; unforgiveness produces death and destruction.

What is forgiveness? It is walking the narrow path. There is no room for reason, excuses, or justification. There is only one narrow path and one narrow gate to get through. There are no exceptions. It is up to me; it is up to you. No one can do it for us, and no one can keep us from doing it. It is a one-person show. There are no other players on stage. No one else is in the courtroom. We are judge, jury, attorney, and recording clerk. What we decide is the decision that stands. There is no appeals court. It is entirely up to you—guilty or acquitted.

You say, "That's too hard. I can't do it." Yes you can. You can make the right decision. You can do the right thing. You have the ability on the inside of you to forgive. Reach down, grab ahold, and choose the right path. If it were easy, everybody would be doing it and everybody would get great results. It may not be easy, but it is definitely not impossible. Many have done it who have had much greater injustices than you. You may think not, but when you get done forgiving, you will see a whole new world of truth.

Let me leave you with this last scripture: Isaiah 35:8-10. It describes a path of freedom, a path of joy, a path of right standing with God. It describes the narrow path of forgiveness. It tells us even a fool will not go astray if he walks this path.

If you have had trouble with unforgiveness, let this

become a lifetime scripture, one you dwell on daily. Let it be your roadmap.

A highway shall be there, and a road, and it shall be called the Highway of Holiness. The unclean shall not pass over it, but it shall be for others. Whoever walks the road, although a fool, shall not go astray.

No lion shall be there, nor shall any ravenous beast go up on it; it shall not be found there. But the redeemed shall walk there,

And the ransomed of the LORD shall return, and come to Zion with singing, with everlasting joy on their heads. They shall obtain joy and gladness, and sorrow and sighing shall flee away.

Isaiah 35:8-10 (NKJ)

CHAPTER FIVE
FORGIVENESS IS—

Parole From Prison

Webster's Dictionary defines the word parole as: 1) a pledged word, especially the promise of a prisoner of war to fulfill stated conditions in return for release, 2) a conditional release of a prisoner before his sentence expires.

In the text of what forgiveness is, parole from prison is a great definition. When we walk in unforgiveness, it is us, and us alone, who confine ourselves to prison. We leave ourselves no choice but to do the time. An old saying goes, "Don't do the crime if you can't do the time." The great part about being placed in prison by our unforgiveness is that we are able at any time to get ourselves paroled.

Let's look at our text, Matthew 18:21-35. We will deal with verses 21 and 22 in detail in the next chapter.

Then Peter came to Him and said, "Lord, how often shall my brother sin against me, and I forgive him? Up to seven times?"

Jesus said to him, "I do not say to you, up to seven times, but up to seventy times seven.

"Therefore the kingdom of heaven is like a certain king who wanted to settle accounts with his servants.

"And when he had begun to settle accounts, one was brought to him who owed him ten thousand talents.

"But as he was not able to pay, his master commanded that he be sold, with his wife and children and all that he had, and that payment be made.

"The servant therefore fell down before him, saying, 'Master, have patience with me, and I will pay you all.'

"Then the master of that servant was moved with compassion, released him, and forgave him the debt.

"But that servant went out and found one of his fellow servants who owed him a hundred denarii; and he laid hands on him and took him by the throat, saying, 'Pay me what you owe!'

"So his fellow servant fell down at his feet and begged him, saying, 'Have patience with me, and I will pay you all.'

"And he would not, but went and threw him into prison till he should pay the debt.

"So when his fellow servants saw what had been done, they were very grieved, and came and told their master all that had been done.

"Then his master, after he had called him, said to him, 'You wicked servant! I forgave you all that debt because you begged me.

'Should you not also have had compassion on your fellow servant, just as I had pity on you?'

"And his master was angry, and delivered him to the torturers until he should pay all that was due to him.

"So My heavenly Father also will do to you if each of you, from his heart, does not forgive his brother his trespasses."

Matthew 18:21-35 (NKJ)

First let's go over this parable. Remember, a parable is "a simple story told to illustrate a moral truth" (Webster's Dictionary). We have a kind King (God) who forgives a great debt that cannot be paid (our sin). Then the servant (you and I) goes out and finds a fellow servant (friend, family, co-worker) and refuses to forgive the debt or even give the other person an opportunity to pay off the debt. With cruelty and unforgiveness he cast the fellow servant into prison until the debt was paid in full. Now we all know you don't exactly make your top wages while confined to prison. This is no position to put someone in if you really want to get paid back.

So when some of the fellow servants saw what was done (this is a good time to remember someone is always watching), they went to the King and told all that was done. You can imagine what you would be thinking if you were in charge. It is mighty upsetting when you go the extra mile to help someone out, and then they go and abuse someone else.

The point is then made that if the King has forgiven you so much, what right do you have not to forgive? God so loved us and sent His Son to die for us so that we could receive full and unlimited forgiveness for what we have done. How could we even have a thought to not forgive another? It is a very foolish man who wants to squash a bug just to be mean when he has just been released from the giant's death grip.

I heard a story many years ago of how to ask for

forgiveness. When we go to someone, we should see ourselves as the mouse under the elephant's foot, presenting our request in as humble a fashion as possible, knowing that at any time the elephant could lower his foot, and we would be finished.

What right do we have to not forgive when we know how much wrong we have done to others? Let no man say he is without sin, for all have sinned and come short of the glory of God. Even a fool, a man who says there is no God, knows that his record is not without blemish. I thank God that blessed are the merciful, for they shall obtain mercy; for surely I could not stand and cast the first stone.

It takes a great amount of pride to be unforgiving toward one who has offended us. The Bible tells us in John, the eighth chapter, about the story of the woman caught in adultery. In the ninth verse it says that no one could cast a stone. Being convicted by their conscience, they went out one by one beginning with the oldest even to the last until all her accusers were gone. Thank God as we get older we should get wiser and be quicker to forgive.

However, this does not seem to be the case, in fact it's just the opposite. Many people, as they get older and the offenses mount up, find it harder and harder to forgive. They leave the narrow path and get on the wide path to destruction. We are told to come to the Lord like a little child, who is so quick to forgive.

A good friend of my father and mother told me not to get involved with children's squabbles. The children will be over it by nightfall, but the parents will continue to fight for years. Here's a story about Fae, Linda, and Becky when they were young. One day they got into a fight and couldn't get along. Unfortunately, the parents got involved and then the fight ensued. It went on for years and years for the parents. They no longer could wave to each other as they passed on the street. No more New Year's Eve celebrations together. Just ugliness and pain.

In fact, it didn't come to an end until folks in the neighborhood died. It took tragedy in two neighborhood families' lives. Too often it takes a disaster to wake us up and bring us back to the reality of life. Fortunately, all the neighbors rallied to help the families who had lost loved ones. The rest of the story is that the three girls all made up and were playing together the next day. The parents argued and fought and lost years of precious friendship. Why lose one more day? It's time to make the choice to forgive. Besides, the meals in prison just aren't that great.

Remember our servant who threw the fellow servant in jail for the small debt. Well, when the king found out, he called the servant, whom he now called wicked, and threw him into prison to be tormented. This sounds like a story you wouldn't want to be a part of.

> *"So likewise shall my heavenly Father do also unto you, if ye from your hearts forgive not every one his brother their trespasses."*
>
> Matthew 18:35

This is no longer a story; this is a sobering thought. Jesus, the Son of God, God in the flesh, says that His Heavenly Father is going to throw you into jail until the debt is paid in full. Now this unforgiveness path has become real serious. This is not like trying to hide something from your mother, a teacher, or a spouse. God does not find out about your sin when you confess it. In fact,

He knows about it before you commit it. This gives Him ample time to complete your cell and line up your tormentors. Do not think that you will escape or be paroled before the debt is paid in full.

Verse 35 says, ". . . If each of you from his heart does not forgive his brother. . . ." Forgiveness has to come from the heart. It cannot be just some words we say like, "I'm sorry. Will you forgive me?"

My favorite passage from the Bible is Proverbs 16:2, which says the ways of a man seem right in his own eyes, BUT God judges the heart, the motive or the intent of man. The truth is that it is somewhat easy to fool a man into thinking what we want him to think. It is never possible to fool God.

We must ask for forgiveness from our heart not from our need. Many times prisoners give an impression that they are rehabilitated, changed, and ready for society, so the parole board lets them out early. All too often they are not changed.

Did the wicked servant go to jail for owing the debt of money? No! He went to jail for his unforgiveness. The good king or a righteous God could not put you into prison for a debt that he had already forgiven. No! He could put him into prison for his new crime which was, according to verse 33, no compassion, no pity.

Going back to the beginning of the text, verses 21 and 22, Peter and Jesus are having a discussion about forgiveness, not financial debt. The new high crime that put this fellow into prison was unforgiveness, not the owing of money. He now remains there until the debt is paid in full. (We will deal with paying the debt shortly; first about prison.)

Prison is a terrible place even if the conditions are good. You are not free to go where you want to go or do what you want to do. You have to eat what they want you to. Worst of all, you can't be with your family, friends, and loved ones.

When we are in unforgiveness, we are in prison. There are places we can't go because so and so might be there. We can't do this because we don't want to have contact with them. When in prison, you might get a visit from someone, but it is short and too far in between. When in unforgiveness, we don't get what we need from those we should be closest to. Most offenses are with the people we are closest to and love the most.

To wrap this chapter up, let's talk about paying the debt. That can only be done by one person. No one can pay this debt for you, not even God. It is all up to you. You will be paroled when your debt is paid. There is only one way—that is for you to forgive. You will remain in that stinky, dingy jail, being tormented until you forgive from your heart. Yes, only one person sits on your parole board. It is you and only you.

Isn't it time for you to get to work, to start again doing something that will make a positive difference in the world in which we live? Ask anyone who has been in prison; you can do more when you are free.

The choice is yours. Only you have the ability to pay the debt. You suffer more than anyone else as a result of your unforgiveness.

FORGIVENESS = PAROLE FROM PRISON.

CHAPTER SIX
FORGIVENESS IS—

A Way of Life

so true

We need to come to a place in life where forgiveness is a way of life, not something we do just when we don't like what someone has done to us. A good test as to whether you have forgiven or not is whether or not you bring up the previous offense. We need to look at this like a banker not a judge.

When you go to see a banker about a debt, he looks at what you currently owe, not what you have paid in the past. This is the right way to look at things when we have been offended. We should not go back and check the old offense account. Have you ever had a repeat offense? Has someone done the same wrong thing to you that they had done to you before? Was it ever you that made the same mistake twice? Let's face it. That happens to all of us as we go through life. Everybody has been a repeat offender at least once.

Let's stop for a moment and take a side journey. Tell me what your parents and teachers were harping on while you were in school, and I will tell you what your boss and your spouse are harping about to you today. Unfortunately, old habits die hard. I am not making any excuses for sin. Sin is sin, and sin is wrong. We should live a holy life, one modeled after Christ's qualities. Still, if you look at it, you have been condemned and ridiculed for years for the same old habits. I bring this up so that we will have compassion when it comes time to forgive and be better able to bear repeated offenses, whether major or minor.

On the other hand, the first thing the judge wants to do is look at your past record. If it is a first-time offense, he is displeased but tends to go easier on you. If you have done it before, things are not going to go so easy for you. Now we have the three strikes law. Three times and you're out. He has no choice but to put you away.

We cannot afford to be the judge of others or set a limit. If you set a limit, you set the situation up for failure. As the judge of the offender, you limited the number of allowable offenses. For some it is one, others three, some ten. When we set a limit, we remind the person this is the last time, which means we have not dealt with and cleaned up the past situations. We are keeping a scorecard. This does not tie in with forgiveness in Matthew 18:21. Peter comes to the Lord and asks Him, "How often shall my brother sin against me and I forgive him? Up to seven times?"

Well, this sounds real spiritual to Peter. He is really stepping out there going for the big seven times. This is two or three times more than many of us have been willing to forgive the faults of others.

Peter may well have been referring to Luke 17:4, where Jesus talked about forgiving seven times a day, or Proverbs 24:16, which states a righteous man may fall seven times and rise again. These are both noble references but nowhere near what God has called us to do. We are too easily focused on limiting our forgiveness, even though we have been forgiven so much.

Matthew 18:22 says, "Jesus said to him, I do not say to you up to seven times, but up to seventy times seven." (70 x 7 = 490) Jesus never desired to set up a specific limit. That is why He gave such a high number, to take off all limits. Any time we set limits, it opens a dangerous door. We start tipping the scales in our favor until we can swing into action and take our revenge. We need to be reminded of Matthew 7:1, "Judge not that you be not judged." We border on making ourselves better than God when we choose to limit our forgiveness to a certain number of offenses. Psalm 78:38 states, "Many a time He turned His anger away." God is so forgiving of us, even though we have done so much. How could we even take a thought of not forgiving?

I want to tell you Pat's story. She has a wonderful husband since he allowed God to change his life, but he wasn't so wonderful the first 11 years of their marriage. His drinking and other nonsense were a constant trial for her. All of that ended except for one bad habit that seemed to turn up about every two years.

Her husband could not hang on to the family cars. Even if the car was paid for, he would end up borrowing money on it, then fall behind in the payments. One night the vehicle was gone. The repo man would strike in the middle of the night. After repossession number eight, Pat could take no more. She said that was enough. Her scale was full, and she could take no more.

At first it was hard to believe. Everything seemed to be going so well. All was coming up roses. They had just come back from a wonderful vacation. They were well rested and ready to hit it again. That Sunday a call came to the house. Pat and her husband had both answered the phone at the same time. Pat's husband was not aware that she had also picked up the phone. The man on the other end of the phone said, "If you don't make your payments, we are coming to get the car." Words that Pat had heard too many times before. To make matters worse, this vehicle was very special to Pat, for a number of reasons.

Well, you know what happened. Pat began to give hubby the third degree. "What's up, you're not going to lose our car, are you? I will never forgive you if you do." Hubby said it would be all right, but he knew in his heart he could not straighten it out.

I gave you all that background to tell you the rest of the story. That night the husband left for work with no intention of ever coming home again. Sounds like a pretty bad man, doesn't it? Not the truth at all. He was a good man who had a recurring problem, and unfortunately, his wife was way beyond her limit. He felt his family would be better off without him. This was not true of course, but he convinced himself it would be best for them.

At first Pat was very angry and upset. How could he get us into this mess again? How unfair could someone be? Then her anger turned to fear when she was faced with the fact that her husband was never coming home again. A mother of four, no money, no job, not knowing what to do.

She began to cry out to God for help and to pray for her husband. After three days God showed Pat she had put a limit on her forgiveness. That night and the next morning

Pat solidified her forgiveness of her husband. Things didn't look any different, but she knew in her heart that she had truly for the first time completely forgiven her husband. The good news is that in less than 12 hours from the completion of her forgiveness, her husband came back home. The reunion was glorious. Pat, for the first time since it all started years ago, could receive her husband and freely love him. There were things to work out, bills to pay, and things to reconcile, but there was something amazingly different from any other time. There was a peace, a love, a joy that had never existed before. Everything ended up being taken care of in a matter of two weeks.

Today Pat's husband has a new car for her and a job with better hours and much more pay. All the back bills are paid off, and their marriage is stronger than ever. The best news though, is Pat's husband has broken the two-year cycle. No more repossessed cars. The power of forgiveness is beyond human ability.

Pat is walking in a lifestyle of forgiveness. There are fewer incidents than ever in their lives. She no longer has a tally sheet, and her husband no longer gives her need for one.

Is forgiveness a way of life for you, or have you become the judge and set up your own three strikes law? Are you capable of clearing the slate?

An important area to work on so we can walk in a life style of forgiveness is forgetting the offenses against us. Boy, just the mention of forgetting will get a rise out of most of us. God, in Psalm 103:12, says He has removed our transgressions from us as far as the east is from the west. Then the cry goes up, "But I'm not God." A good thought for a side journey, since you are now in a humble moment. This is the time for you to make a decision to quit taking charge of your own life. With God in charge, it will open up a whole new world of possibilities, for with Him all things are possible. We certainly can't do it on our own. We have proven that. What we need to do is get started on this path.

Let's make this process simpler for you. Instead of forgetting the whole incident all at once, cry out to God for the grace to get started. Allow yourself the liberty to start to forgive. Don't even take the thought, "What if it happens again?" Step out. Begin to love with God's love. You may not be able to forget the incident right now, but your forgiveness will allow your pain to be healed, and the worst part will be forgotten.

John 16:21 (NKJ) tells us:

"A woman when she is in labor, has sorrow because her hour has come; but as soon as she has given birth to the child, she no longer remembers the anguish, for joy that a human being has been born into the world."

Once we have given birth to forgiveness, we can put that incident behind us. Our mind will be free to create since it is not busy destroying.

There is so much pain in our life when we cannot come to forgiveness. Perhaps it is time to make forgiveness a lifestyle like breathing or eating. It is something that needs to be done for our benefit. Is it time for you to go toe to toe with God, to birth that forgiveness, to be able to put those painful memories behind you once and for all?

FORGIVENESS IS A WAY OF LIFE.

CHAPTER SEVEN
HOW TO FORGIVE—

It Starts With Love

Forgiveness is the most powerful force I have ever known or seen. I have seen it immediately obtain the desired result. People have waited for years, tried all kinds of ways, means, and methods, and then they forgave. This opens a door so wide that nothing can stop the manifestation. What a wonderful thing to see people leap out of bondage into their full potential!

Remember, unforgiveness puts us in prison, which hinders us from coming to our greatest results. No matter what we can accomplish in prison, we can do abundantly more out of prison.

After thinking on forgiveness, reading the testimonies, and crying out to God for the answer, it is now clear to me that forgiveness is a part of love. Forgiveness is love. Love forgives! In 1 Corinthians 13:4-8 these descriptions of love keep spelling out forgiveness. We will take a look at each phrase and break it down.

Love suffers long. To walk in forgiveness, we must be willing to suffer offenses. Many times offenses go on for a long time. Unforgiveness is not willing to suffer long. It sometimes takes the offense immediately and other times sets a limit. Neither one works with love and forgiveness. When we walk in forgiveness, we deal with our own character flaws and receive grace to cover the faults of others.

Love is kind. It takes a kind person to forgive. A kind person considers others and their needs, not themselves. When we are kind to someone, it becomes very difficult to take an offense. Forgiveness desires to actively create contributions for other people's lives. Forgiveness looks for ways to give without expecting a return.

Love does not envy. James 3:16, states "For where envy and self seeking exist, confusion and every evil thing are there." Sounds like the fruit of unforgiveness. A person who does not follow the teachings of Jesus is spelled out in 1 Timothy 6:4, "He is proud, knowing nothing, but is obsessed with disputes and arguments over words, from which come envy, strife, reviling, evil suspicions." This verse describes a person who is in unforgiveness. Love forgives, and when we forgive, we love. No forgiveness, no love, but certainly plenty of envy. Forgiveness is not jealous or possessive. Forgiveness rejoices in another's victory.

Love doesn't parade itself. When we walk in unforgiveness we have to fight for our own spot and make sure we are taken care of. Forgiveness knows that the blessings always flow. Those who forgive will receive in due season if they faint not (don't take an offense). Forgiveness does not have to be right and prove the other wrong.

Love is not puffed up. When unforgiveness is involved, we like to point the finger at the other guy. We take the wide road and make excuses. Pride comes from insecurity. Forgiveness gives you confidence; unforgiveness makes you puffed up. Forgiveness does not use belittling remarks to harm others. Forgiveness does not seek its own.

Love does not behave rudely. People in unforgiveness are not polite or easy to get along with. They don't care about others, but they are concerned for themselves. People who forgive treat others with fairness and kindness. They are flexible, willing to flow and not forcing their way on others.

Love does not seek its own. When we do not forgive, we are looking for our own. What's in it for me? You owe me. When we take an offense, we must start to take care of ourselves. Forgiveness allows God to take care of us. Vengeance is mine, says the Lord. So while God is dealing with our enemies and taking care of us and all our needs, we are free to forgive, able to be creative and give to others. We don't have to take a thought for our own needs. Those with unforgiveness expect life to revolve around them.

Love is not provoked. Have you ever noticed that once you have taken an offense, it does not matter what the offender does? You are provoked. They walk in a room, and you get upset. They say hello, and you go on the defensive. Every word is heard as a word of offense. When we are blinded by our offense, we are unable to see any good thing the offender does. Forgiving people are not provoked. They are able to see beyond the action, to see the hurt of the person and be compassionate, not taking things personally.

Love thinks no evil. Love and forgiveness do not think "here we go again" when they meet someone who has done them wrong in the past. Forgiveness thinks good thoughts: "That's over, now we can go on. I knew they could make it." Unforgiveness is looking for another fight, the next slip-up to be made. Unforgiveness is believing for the worst and usually getting it. Unforgiveness wants to complain because it mainly has been thinking on evil things. Forgiveness overlooks the failures of others and goes on.

Love does not rejoice in iniquity. When we have forgiven someone, we don't get frustrated when we see them out of fellowship with God or man. It is good when the brethren dwell together in unity. Unforgiveness likes to find one more person who thinks like they do about the offender. Then they can get out the barbecue and have a roast together. Unforgiving people have taken an offense and then have a unique ability to find each other and rejoice in the iniquity of the mutual offender. Forgiveness is not being a talebearer or a gossip.

Love rejoices in the truth. Unforgiveness does not want to hear the truth, let alone rejoice in it. Remember Fred, who got bitter with his boss over the lost bonus? His two friends told him the truth in love. Fred said it was a good word, but he wanted to get even with his boss. When we walk in forgiveness, we are hungry for the truth. The truth is desired because that is what sets us free and keeps us free. A wise man receives reproof because he knows it is truth. Forgiveness rejoices in the success of others.

Love bears all things. Strong's Concordance (#4722) tells us this means to roof over, i.e. (figuratively), to cover over with silence (endure patiently). Forgiveness can forgive, forget, and move on. Unforgiveness wants to bring it up over and over and over. There is no end to it. Unforgivers not only want to throw it in the face of the offender, but it is a topic of discussion with fellow offendees and many times accompanied with the words, "I have already dealt with that." If it is over, it is unlikely to come up again. If it does come up, there should be no pain or ill feeling associated with it. Remember, forgiveness is a powerful force. It gives us a strength that cannot be comprehended, an ability to bear up under a load that would crush most others, and a strength to bear all things, strength beyond human reason. Forgiveness covers the weaknesses and shortcomings of others.

Love believes all things. Forgiveness believes all things. This word, believe, means "to place confidence in, to trust." When we have forgiven someone, we trust them; we place our confidence in them. I know what you're thinking—I will forgive them but no way will I trust them again. Forgiveness and trust go hand in hand when there is a true restoration.

People have marveled at how I can forgive someone and even think about having confidence in them, let alone trust them. There have been people I was extremely close with who would turn and say and do all manner of evil against me. They take an offense, and can no longer think straight. I choose to forgive them before they ever take an opportunity to ask for forgiveness. When and if they come to the truth, I am able to restore them in spite of any mean things said or done to me.

Forgiving is God's way, and we are commanded to follow it. Forgiveness does not stumble or quit because of the inconsistencies of others. This is the way to get people set free, to truly, without reserve, forgive them.

Let me plug in Tanya's story here. She did not get total release the first, the third, or even the twenty-third time. She did get it, however, because she was fully forgiven, which included full restoration each and every time she faltered until she finally became completely free. Remember, love and forgiveness never fail. Here is Tanya's story in her own words:

I was between the ages of nine and thirteen when my path and course of life were already determined. Because of the many misfortunes that had happened to me during these tender years and not knowing the love and forgiveness of God, I began to hate myself and of course placed the blame on my parents.

I became driven by some unknown force that was in me. The more I hated and the more bitter I became, the more I was driven by this force of destruction. The root of bitterness, resentment, and unforgiveness that I had carried in my heart had fully birthed itself in me. It was determined to control my destiny. I turned to drugs and pills. I became so consumed that I didn't care what happened to me, whom I hurt or whom I destroyed, including myself and specifically the men and women of authority in my life.

At this young age I started sleeping with any man who showed an interest in me. The more someone wanted to love me, the more I was determined to destroy him. I started drinking, not knowing how to deal with the pain, guilt, and shame. From that time on I was an alcoholic, harlot, and full-blown drug addict. I was on my way to hell in a handbasket and taking as many with me as I could. I can't express enough how ugly, miserable, and lost I was and the terrible devastating consequences it had brought in my life.

I had an abortion at age 13, moved away from home at 18, was married at age 20, and divorced before I was 30. I continued in improper sexual activities, resulting in several female infections and other problems, including severe scar tissue. It all ended in my being unable to have children.

I went through a very traumatic divorce and had even destroyed my own husband. I lost everything— my home, my husband, and by this time all self-worth. I was a complete failure. If it were not for God, I honestly believe that I would be dead today.

With no hope left, I was invited to church by a friend. It was then that I was taken up under the wings of two very wonderful and wise people in my life. Here is where I learned my true destiny. I was discipled, trained, and loved. I had to learn how to forgive and truly love, and it was hard for me to be honest with myself and God. It has been a process for me and sometimes very painful. But I didn't quit. I've learned that "winners never quit."

That once perverted and destructive drive in me has been purified, and I've been made whole. I praise God for His saving grace. My new drive is only to know Christ more. I give God all the glory for opening my eyes and teaching me His love, mercy, and forgiveness. God has and still is restoring back to me all that the devil has stolen. I have a wonderful husband, who is a man of God, a beautiful home, two precious children, and still so much more to come.

I still have to deal with offenses, for they will always come. The difference now is I win. No matter what the circumstance is or looks like, I am the victor and I'm free.

— Tanya Carter

It took someone to believe in Tanya to keep restoring her. She needed to know the love of God. She needed to know she was forgiven. She would be dead if she had not been forgiven. How many failures in life could be avoided, shipwrecks averted if only we could forgive and believe in them?

Love hopes all things. The word hope here means to expect. The trouble with life is you get what you expect. This word hope stresses the character of those who "hope" more than the action of hope. It shows the character of the one expecting.

General George S. Patton, the most successful and unforgettable general of WWII, was known for getting the job done. He had an expectation of his troops, and they didn't let him down (19 Stars, page 233). The men of the third army were ordinary human beings. They were inexperienced and unschooled in war. They were not volunteers. Yet they fought with a morale and spirit that made them one of the most successful armies in WWII. "Patton," said an officer "had the ability to deliver that indefinable something which makes men want to go out and give their all for him; to do just a little bit more than it is humanly possible to do." General Patton was able to hope for the best, and he got it.

Look at your relationships. You will see that you get what you have been expecting—not necessarily what you wanted but what you expected. How many times have you said, "I knew it, I knew it. I tried to tell you." These are words heard when the wrong thing was expected.

Forgiveness expects the best. Unforgiveness expects something less and too many times the worst. Forgiveness does not quit on a relationship when things go wrong. Those who forgive stick with relationships, look for the best, and find it.

Love endures all things. To endure is to keep going. It is so easy to give up, especially if we are trying to do it on our own. Forgiveness has to keep going; it cannot quit. To endure takes a deep love, a lifestyle of forgiving. It has to be a way of thinking, a way of life. Otherwise we are one thought away from unforgiveness, one thought away from quitting, one thought away from giving ourselves a prison sentence. Forgiveness can overcome anything and endure even if it is not accepted or returned.

Love never fails. Forgiveness never fails. Forgiveness is the secret ingredient that is missing from most of life's failures. One bad decision leads to another bad decision. Trouble starts with one offense, and before you know it, we have three divorces and are working on the fourth. Forgiveness never stops or comes to its limit no matter how hard things are going.

Keep yourself on the alert as to whom you need to forgive and whom you are holding back. Whom do you need to go to and ask forgiveness so you can be forgiven and thrust forward? Be reminded that when we judge someone, we are guilty of that thing ourselves (Romans 2:1).

How do we forgive? We start by walking in the love of God that has been shed abroad in our hearts. If you don't have that love, you back up one step and ask Jesus to be the Lord of your life. Open up your heart and let Him in. Then you will be able to forgive, let go, and never be bothered with it again. Since to forgive is to let it go, I want to close this chapter with the words of a song called, "Let It Go" by the Super Mega Tones, a Christian singing group out of Sacramento, California.

After reading the words, be sure you have let it go!

Every day of your life
You'll have a chance to get into strife
Think about when somebody does you wrong
What do you do? What do you do?
We're going to try to tell you with our song
What to do? What to do?
Every day of your life?
You'll have a chance to get into strife
The lady in the checkout line's too slow
Let it go Let it go
Impatience only hurts yourself you know
So let it go Just let it go
Every day of your life
You'll have a chance to get into strife
The people around you don't know how to drive
Let it go Just let it go
Holding your temper could keep you alive
So let it go Just let it go
Every day of your life
You'll have a chance to get into strife
Think about when somebody does you wrong
Let it go Just let it go
That's what we tried to tell you with our song
To let it go Please let it go
Let it go Let it go Let it go
Just let it go!

CHAPTER EIGHT
FORGIVENESS IS—

Like an Onion

Wouldn't it be great if we could wave the gospel wand and everything we need could be done in a moment? Well, you have lived life and you know that isn't true. Many times things have to be done in stages. This is not an excuse for slowing the process and taking longer to deal with an issue than is needed. We will say more about delaying things at the end of the chapter.

Perhaps this is a good time for you to stop, set the book down, and peel an onion. That's right. Don't slice it or dice it. Peel it one layer at a time. If you are not willing to do it right now, be sure to do it soon. The illustration of the onion will help you to expand your understanding of forgiveness.

I just finished peeling my own onion. I logged my thoughts and my time. It took me twenty-one minutes to peel the onion and four minutes to wash my hands, blow my nose, and take out the trash. I used a medium-sized yellow onion. The only side effects are that my eyes are a little sore and teary and my hands have a very slight onion smell.

When we have not been living a life of forgiveness, it is just like our onion. There is a thin, hard outer layer that gives protection to what is inside. It is a little difficult to get started peeling, but then it comes off in big chunks. Forgiveness is the same way—hard to get started, but once you get going, it goes in big chunks. When I finished with the first layer, it was a different color and a little smaller but still the same shape. When forgiveness is under way, we will look different though basically still the same. Many times our forgiveness will come in layers. God does not give us more than we can bear.

I remember March of 1977 well. After being filled to overflowing with His Spirit and His love, I went through a month of accelerated, dramatic changes. I lost 35 pounds and 30 bad habits in 30 days. It was an exciting time. Each morning as I woke up, I would spend time in prayer and waiting on the Lord. I would receive fresh instruction daily. In the first days God would show me a person I needed to go to, either to forgive or to obtain forgiveness. By the end of the month I was seeing two or more persons per day. It was at that point that my wife would say, "Who are you going to see today?" It was a glorious time of healing and deliverance. Someone asked one time if I really was delivered of 30 bad habits. I went home that day, sat down with my wife, and we easily filled up the list with over 30.

God will deal with us as much and as quickly as we will let Him. He also will never give us more than we can bear. Not too long after this month of great deliverance took place in my life, I observed this guy who was more than most would care to deal with. I asked my wife if I used to be that bad. She said, "Oh no, you were a lot worse!" Because of God's grace I did not know how bad I was. If I had known, I probably would have shot myself, because in my miserable days I would not have put up with somebody like that, especially myself.

You would think that after 30 days of intense healing I was pretty well set. That was true for the past hurts and disappointments of my life, then the maturing process began I had forgiven and been forgiven. Through everyday events I had to learn to walk a continual daily path of forgiveness. Now forgiveness is a way of life. *For me too*

The forgiveness onion being peeled has given God all these years to keep peeling other onions of change. It takes a lifetime to build a man. It cannot be done in one day. Daily we need to allow God the liberty to work in our lives, ever molding, shaping, and peeling, taking us to ever greater heights.

Back to my onion peeling. I noted that each layer was harder to start and more difficult to peel. By the time I got to the fifth layer, my eyes were tearing up.

When we start out, God works on the obvious things, the exterior layers like smoking, drinking, and stealing. You would think they would be hard, but by God's grace they are easy. As time goes on, God starts peeling down to the things that others can't necessarily see, things not close to the surface but surely there. We have closely guarded them in our hidden layers, concealing them below the surface of everyday living. A few tears, a little objection, and then they're gone.

By the seventh layer, things looked the same, no change in color or shape, just smaller in size. We have unforgiveness and situations that have been hidden deep in the vault. You know those things that people have been trying to get you to admit to but you keep finding an excuse to slip out of it. I have found a pattern that many people follow to freedom if they take it all the way through:

1. They deny they have the problem.

2. They start to see the problem.

3. They know the problem is there but deny it is a problem.

4. Okay, so it is a problem but you should love me while you are dealing with it.

5. Okay it's a problem. It's up to me, and I am going to deal with it.

6. I'm dealing with it and have an occasional slip back.

7. I'm free, it's over, and I am glad it's all behind me.

Wouldn't it be great if we would all humble ourselves, go to the onion factory, get peeled, and be done with it?

A good note to take: Listen to what people have been telling you for years. You heard it from your parents, then your teachers, now it's your spouse and your friends. It is not a plot against you. It would do you good to listen and get set free.

For years I remember people telling me I had this harsh look in my eyes. After my life got straightened out it was not as often, but I still heard about it. I always denied it and said people were reading me wrong. One day I went to a photographer who did not know me well. He told me I had this harsh look in my eyes. I knew he had nothing to gain by telling me this, so I listened. It was true. Everyone had been right. I had not felt or thought the way people were seeing me look, but the look was there. Thank God for that photographer. He told me if "it" was all right, he could work that look out of me in this one session. I said, "Go for it, please." The rest is history. That look is not there anymore because I realized it, faced it, and dealt with it.

A tip for those who are trying to help someone you love get free of something they don't see or won't see. They tell you many times you are judging them, therefore they don't want to listen to you. The truth is many times you are judging them, if not in that area then in other areas. Judgment of another jeopardizes your ability to help them. Make sure you are saying it in love and for their benefit. It is usually easier to pray and ask God to put someone else across their path to tell them. There will be no ax to grind or benefit to gain, so listening and doing come easier when it comes from someone not as close to us.

Back to the onion. After peeling the ninth layer my onion was in two pieces, one large piece and another small one. The two pieces sat on the bottom of the onion leaning to one side. I was getting close to the heart. The small piece came off easily. It was not so tough. Nothing quite like a quick, easy victory.

Many times when we are in the forgiving process, we take out a chunk, and we think as a result we have the victory. What will happen is we end up putting off, sometimes for years, the final victory. Keep pressing in, because the finale is close at hand. Don't let the small piece fool you even though it seems to be enough. There is still more to do.

The tenth layer was a thick layer and a slimy one. See, we are getting close to the mother lode. We want to slip on by, but no, we press in.

The eleventh layer begins to come off in big chunks. I ended up with two pieces, teardrop in shape, one larger, the other much smaller. They were both attached to the base or root. You are close now, right at the heart of the matter. You are closer than ever to the great victory. You have been through a lot, but you have made it. Only two to go.

The little one snapped right off. It was just barely attached to the base. Don't be sidetracked by the victory. Keep pressing in. It is an important step; it needs to be done. Now you are down to the core, the last battle before your total victory.

The thirteenth and final layer I found firmly attached to the base, unlike the last one. I had to add pressure to force the issue. I heard a snap of victory. I was able to throw the base and the last of it into the trash. When you make it to the core of your onion, it is a great day. You have pressed to a place of forgiveness that many fear to face. You are now on the narrow path, ready to receive an abundance of blessings.

It is a spiritual battle; the enemy wants to fight us at every layer. He lies to us at each new layer saying, "That's enough, that's all there is. You are all done." Don't buy the lie. Keep walking forward. You don't have to go on a witch-hunt looking for something to be wrong. The key is to stay open. If you stay on the path, it will automatically happen. Remember, it is a narrow path and you won't get lost.

In the beginning of the chapter I mentioned delays in

the forgiveness process. There are layers to deal with, and it must be done in God's time. However, when God shows us something, many like to say they are working on it. This can be an excuse to gain credit by works. If the price has been paid—and it has—then the price has been paid. If we have been shown what is wrong, then deal with it and give God the glory. Many times the phrase "I am working on it" is an excuse to keep walking in unforgiveness or a desire to earn our forgiveness. Both would be wrong.

Think of how many things you have already changed in life, many of them bigger than what you are facing now. Make no excuses. Go forward. Be all you can be. Stay on the timetable of God instead of what's comfortable for you.

So how do we forgive? One step at a time, just like peeling an onion. Don't get in a hurry. Take it one day at a time. Don't box yourself in. Be patient, and it will all work out.

In the forgiveness process, when you go to someone to get forgiveness, to say you're sorry, please, for your benefit and theirs, get them to say, "I forgive you." Too many times people want to blow it off, saying, "There's no need for this" or "I don't know what you are talking about." Explain to them that it is very important to you. Have them tell you, "I forgive you." This will help you tremendously.

Sometimes these people are working things out in their own life. There is also great potential for opening up doors in their life. There is something very satisfying and completing about hearing those words, "I forgive you."

Don't just rush on by, say you're sorry, and leave it at that. You have come this far with it; don't leave it half undone. Also, don't do it in writing, do it in person. The written word can sometimes be used against you. The scripture says when you have ought with your brother, go to him. When you go to him, you can be face-to-face, eyeball to eyeball. The phone can suffice but should be used when great distances make the other unreasonable.

You're now on the narrow road, and that leads only to blessings.

CHAPTER NINE
HOW TO FORGIVE

This chapter is for everyone but dedicated to those of you who have the most difficult time dealing with unforgiveness.

It will be a lot easier for you when you realize that forgiveness is not an option, that unforgiveness brings great devastation to our lives. Forgiveness is as important to us as breathing. Without air we cannot live. Without forgiveness we shall surely die. When we don't forgive, we pay a big price. Here is Pam's story:

I was just about to turn 13 when I was deeply hurt by my best friend and her parents. I didn't know what I had done to make them hurt me so. Before this happened I was a very happy, cheerful teenager. After their betrayal I became depressed. I no longer trusted people, not even my close friends. This lasted for about three years, and during those years I became more bitter and began to hate more people. I was not enjoying the way my life was. I was miserable, and I wanted everyone around me to be miserable.

Then one afternoon as I was sitting in my bedroom, I realized that this bitterness was holding me back from what I was called to do. If I would just forgive them, I would be a lot happier and able to go on and receive the blessings of forgiveness.

I wrote to her and asked for her forgiveness. This inspired her to write me back to forgive me and also ask for my forgiveness. We have now been writing for the last four years, not best friends but back in fellowship. In the last four years I have opened up to other relationships. I am now happy with myself and am helping other teens and children receive the blessings of forgiveness.

It is no fun being miserable and alone. Let's look at some scriptures that will help us be convinced of the need to forgive:

Not returning evil for evil or reviling for reviling, but on the contrary blessing, knowing that you were called to this, that you may inherit a blessing.

1 Peter 3:9 (NKJ)

In this verse we see that forgiveness gives us inheritance rights to a blessing. When we forgive someone who has wronged us, we put ourselves in position for a blessing. We all need more blessings in our lives, and forgiveness will keep them flowing. Unforgiveness will block them in a hurry. Forgiveness will open the floodgate.

Here is Tim and Stacie's story of putting themselves back into position for a blessing.

We purchased a car on a lease option with a $500 cash down payment. Then we changed our mind and decided to finance it through our credit union. In order to do that, the seller would have to drop the price $1200. We already had the car, and they refused to come down in price. After getting counsel we decided to take the car back even though it had been 30 days. They said, "There is no way we will give you your $500 back. As a matter of fact, you owe us for driving the car for a month."

About a week passed, with us, mostly me, fuming and letting it affect my whole life. I went to a church meeting on Thursday where my pastor reminded me to just forgive them, release it, and go on. So I did. It was not long before Stacie and I had a $500 check come in the mail with a letter of apology from the company. I am so glad my eyes were opened and the blessings unblocked.

It is astounding what can happen and how quickly it can turn around when we forgive.

Matthew 5:7 says, "Blessed are the merciful, for they shall obtain mercy." I have never met anyone who does not need mercy. Take a short time to list your own shortcomings and failures. Now that you have the list in front of you, look it over. Do you have any room to deny another the mercy you need?

While you have your list in front of you and it's fresh on your mind, let's look at Matthew 6:12 and 6:14-15.

And forgive us our debts, as we forgive our debtors.

Matthew 6:12 (NKJ)

For if you forgive men their trespasses, your heavenly Father will also forgive you.

But if you do not forgive men their trespasses, neither will your Father forgive your trespasses.

Matthew 6:14-15 (NKJ)

We will be forgiven as we have forgiven, and more

importantly, God can only forgive us if we forgive. If we do not forgive, God cannot forgive us. Knowing how much we need forgiveness, I personally would not want to be unforgiving and force God into a place where He could not forgive me. If for any reason your list was too short for you to realize you need forgiveness, pass the list to your family and friends. They will surely be able to lengthen it for you.

> *And be kind to one another, tenderhearted, forgiving one another, just as God in Christ forgave you.*
>
> Ephesians 4:32 (NKJ)

> *Bearing with one another, and forgiving one another, if anyone has a complaint against another; even as Christ forgave you, so you also must do.*
>
> Colossians 3:13 (NKJ)

It is very clear that we are commanded to forgive. John 14:15 tells us, "If you love Me, keep My commandments." Do we love God? If so, then we must keep His commandments. We are commanded to live in forgiveness. Since we love God, we must forgive.

Remember that forgiveness is not a feeling, it is a choice. We do it by faith. We get started, and God's grace kicks in. We don't have to do it on our own; the Father will help us.

Another reason to walk in forgiveness is that unforgiveness puts us with the wrong crowd. We will begin with Romans 1:17-31.

> *For in it the righteousness of God is revealed from faith to faith; as it is written, "The just shall live by faith."*

> *For the wrath of God is revealed from heaven against*

all ungodliness and unrighteousness of men, who suppress the truth in unrighteousness,

because what may be known of God is manifest in them, for God has shown it to them.

For since the creation of the world His invisible attributes are clearly seen, being understood by the things that are made, even His eternal power and Godhead, so that they are without excuse,

because, although they knew God, they did not glorify Him as God, nor were thankful, but became futile in their thoughts, and their foolish hearts were darkened.

Professing to be wise, they became fools,

and changed the glory of the incorruptible God into an image made like corruptible man—and birds and four-footed animals and creeping things.

Therefore God also gave them up to uncleanness, in the lusts of their hearts, to dishonor their bodies among themselves,

who exchanged the truth of God for the lie, and worshiped and served the creature rather than the Creator, who is blessed forever. Amen.

For this reason God gave them up to vile passions. For even their women exchanged the natural use for what is against nature.

Likewise also the men, leaving the natural use of the woman, burned in their lust for one another, men with men committing what is shameful, and receiving in themselves the penalty of their error which was due.

And even as they did not like to retain God in their knowledge, God gave them over to a debased mind, to do those things which are not fitting;

being filled with all unrighteousness, sexual immorality, wickedness, covetousness, maliciousness; full of envy, murder, strife, deceit, evil-mindedness; they are whisperers,

backbiters, haters of God, violent, proud, boasters, inventors of evil things, disobedient to parents,

*undiscerning, untrustworthy, unloving, **unforgiving**, unmerciful . . .*

Romans 1:17-31 (NKJ)

The scripture tells us that everything is established by two or three witnesses. Here is another list.

But know this, that in the last days perilous times will come:

*For men will be lovers of themselves, lovers of money, boasters, proud, blasphemers, disobedient to parents, unthankful, unholy, unloving, **unforgiving**, slanderers, without self-control, brutal, despisers of good, traitors, headstrong, haughty, lovers of pleasures rather than lovers of God,*

having a form of godliness but denying its power. And from such people turn away!

2 Timothy 3:1-5 (NKJ)

This is not a list on which we would like to be. Unforgiveness is listed in both references with some mighty ugly problems, things that most of us would not want to be associated with. In fact in 2 Timothy 3:5 it says, "from such people turn away." In Romans 1:20 it says that we are without excuse. No attorney or loophole will get us out of this. We will not be able to stand before God and say, "But you don't know what they did to me." God knows what they did, and He shows us in these verses what group we are a part of if we do not walk in forgiveness.

Let's finish looking at these verses and see in Romans 1:32 and 2:1 why we do not forgive, and why we tend to judge someone else for what they do wrong.

Who, knowing the righteous judgment of God, that those who practice such things are deserving of death, not only do the same but also approve of those who practice them.

Romans 1:32 (NKJ)

Therefore you are inexcusable, O man, whoever you are who judge, for in whatever you judge another you condemn yourself; for you who judge practice the same things.

Romans 2:1 (NKJ)

It is very clear in these verses that we have no excuses for judging and that we are guilty of the very things for which we judge another for. Whenever you see or hear people judging others, it will be clear what the accusers are guilty of themselves. The scripture says it, and it is absolutely true. What we judge another for we are guilty of ourselves! To walk in unforgiveness we have to judge. To judge another, we must be guilty of it ourselves.

Over 20 years ago I smoked two packs of cigarettes a day. Thank God I'm free! Since I have been healed and set free I do not have to condemn smokers. I don't like smoking, and I do not encourage it. However, I am patient with those who are still in the process of getting free. Those in the church who judge smokers, even those who never smoked, are guilty themselves. They may not be guilty of smoking, but they have some habit that makes them guilty so that they have to judge.

This is a great warning sign, if we will use it as such. Whenever we find ourselves judging someone, we need to open up and see where it exists in our own life. The scripture is true that says, "For you who judge practice the same thing."

I trust this gives you plenty of ammunition to want to forgive. We will now go into some more practical steps of how to forgive.

Matthew 5:44 tells us to bless, do good, and pray. Remember, anything God asks us to do He will help us to complete it.

We will start off with **blessing those who curse you**. These are odd words, but the scripture tells us God's ways are not our ways. We must adopt God's ways if we want the good life. Something happens to us on the inside when we do good things for those who have done bad things to us. When we invest, we increase. By blessing those who have done you wrong, you get free. Besides, a curse cannot fall on a righteous man. It's also fun to watch other people's amazement when they are startled by our ability to bless instead of curse.

Do good to those who hate you. It can be the most aggravating thing you can do, when you are good to those who hate you. You see, they want you to become like them. If you hate back, then you end up joining their ranks, becoming just like them. They can't handle forgiveness. It will either bring them to a place of repentance or a state of confusion that renders them harmless. When you do good, it keeps you in the driver's seat. You are the leader, not the follower. Unforgiveness will place a ring in your nose to lead you around wherever hate decides to lead you. No longer free to make your own decisions, you are driven by hate. Romans 12:21 tells us, "Do not be overcome by evil, but overcome evil with good." When you do good, you overcome hate.

Pray for those who spitefully use you. This is the master key to forgiveness. It will open every locked heart, no matter how many chains or what size the lock. The number or depth of the wounds cannot stop forgiveness from coming if we pray for those who spitefully use us. When we begin to pray for that person, a most powerful course is embarked upon.

While praying we become intimate with the One we pray to, the one we pray for, and the one we pray with. The one we pray to, of course, is Almighty God. When you are intimate with Him, you are intimate with the best. Because you are intimate with God, you spend time with Him. Spending time with Him causes you to become like Him. God is always ready to forgive.

> *"I, even I, am He who blots out your transgressions for My own sake; And I will not remember your sins."*
>
> Isaiah 43:25 (NKJ)

This is our most powerful scripture yet. I repeat, we become intimate with the One we pray to—intimacy causes us to be like Him. This verse tells us He blots out our sin. We can forgive also because we are like Him. The verse says that God forgave for His own sake. The biggest result comes in us when we forgive. We must forgive for our sake. It is not wrong for us to benefit; in fact, we are better able to help others.

Last, but not least, God has no remembrance. We dealt with this earlier, and it is worth repeating. We can forget the pain at a minimum. When the pain is healed, it is forgotten. We do not have to keep bringing it up every day. It can be over.

Here is Heather's story. In her own words she tells us how she used the master key to unlock her forgiveness.

I always thought I was a very forgiving person until somebody hurt me so badly I thought that life, as I knew it, was over. For months, I wouldn't even consider forgiving this person. I didn't want to forgive them, and I never wanted to see their face again as long as I lived. I wanted them to hurt every day, every minute, as badly as I hurt.

The months became a year and then even longer. Soon, I trusted no one. I became unforgiving and bitter towards people that hadn't even hurt me. I was suspicious of everybody. I knew the only way to get past this was to pray for the person I considered my number one enemy.

I didn't want to pray for them, bless them, or do good to them, but I knew that this was my only way out. I got my *Prayers That Avail Much* out and sat there and wept. I couldn't pray out loud. But God saw my first step. Day after day I would pray and cry as I read the prayer of forgiveness for myself and this person.

God truly worked a miracle in my heart. It didn't take long before I truly began to love this person again. Now I have absolutely no resentment, unforgiveness, or bitterness with this person.

God truly is the restorer when we do things this way. He has set out the blueprint for forgiveness in His Word, and when we follow it, we can walk in love with those who have hurt us. We will never lose by loving. God will never short us; He has a way for us to overcome. *so true Thank you Jesus*

What a powerful testimony of how praying for those who spitefully use us will set us free! *Free to be myself*

We need to at least touch on how to pray for those who spitefully use us. We cannot start praying that they die or move away. We need to pray out of a heart of compassion. As you can see from Heather's testimony, she had to start by faith. She needed to use a prayer that had been written out by someone else. This is fine. In fact, I have reprinted prayer number 12, "To Walk in Forgiveness," from the *Prayers That Avail Much* that Heather used.

TO WALK IN FORGIVENESS

Father, in the name of Jesus, I make a fresh commitment to You to live in peace and harmony, not only with the other brothers and sisters of the Body of Christ, but also with my friends, associates, neighbors, and family.

I let go of all bitterness, resentment, envying, strife, and unkindness in any form. I give no place to the devil, in Jesus' name. Now Father, I ask Your forgiveness. By faith, I receive it, having assurance that I am cleansed from all unrighteousness through Jesus Christ. I ask You to forgive and release all who have wronged and hurt me. I forgive and release them. Deal with them in your mercy and loving-kindness.

From this moment on, I purpose to walk in love, to seek peace, to live in agreement, and to conduct myself toward others in a manner that is pleasing to You. I know that I have right standing with You and Your ears are attentive to my prayers. *amen*

It is written in Your Word that the love of God has been poured forth into my heart by the Holy Ghost who is given to me. I believe that love flows forth into the lives of everyone I know, that I may be filled with and abound in the fruits of righteousness which bring glory and honor unto You, Lord, in Jesus' name. So be it!

Scripture References: Romans 12:10, 16-18; 1 Peter 3:8, 11-12; Philippians 2:2; Colossians 1:10; Romans 5:5; John 1:9; Philippians 1:11; Mark 11:25; Ephesians 4:27, 31-32.

As each day passed, Heather obtained more healing until the day of her freedom came and all resentment was gone. She prayed not a bitter prayer but a prayer of truth, which became a prayer of love.

Another prayer right out of scripture is Ephesians 3:14-21. It is a prayer for inner growth. You fill in the blanks.

For this reason I bow my knees to the Father of our Lord Jesus Christ, from whom the whole family in heaven and earth is named, that He would grant **JoAnn Dennis** *, according to the riches of His glory, to be strengthened with might through His Spirit in the inner man, that Christ may dwell in* **JoAnn Dennis** *'s heart* *through faith; that _JoAnn Dennis_, being rooted and grounded in love, may be able to comprehend with all the saints what is the width and length and depth and height—to know the love of Christ which passes knowledge; that _JoAnn Dennis_ may be filled with all the fullness of God. Now to Him who is able to do exceedingly abundantly above all that we ask or think, according to the power that works in us, to Him be glory in the church by Christ Jesus to all generations, forever and ever. Amen.*

If you will pray this prayer each day for you and your offender, you will see quick, miraculous results in both of you.

It doesn't have to take a long time. God is willing to work as fast as you are willing to go. Many times it is we who speed up or slow down the process.

Here is Janet's story:

Our son was in grade school, and we had been using drugs for some time. One of those dark nights we had an awful fight and put him in the middle of it. We were literally pulling him in two directions, each of us screaming that we would claim him when we split up. When we came to our senses, we all talked about it and asked for forgiveness. We thought it was over, but this was not the end.

Months passed and our son went to spend some time with Grandpa and Grandma during Christmas vacation. My husband and I had just finished a time of prayer, asking God to help us in our attempt to stop using drugs, when the phone rang. It was Grandma telling us that she and Grandpa were on their way over to talk to us about something.

As soon as they arrived, Grandma lit into us. She was really upset because of what we were doing to our son. Our son had shared with her what had taken place during the big fight that dark night. Her words were motivated by anger, and a lot of unkind and untrue things were said.

When they left that evening, I had a fear rise up inside of me like I'd never known before. I feared her taking our son away from us. It was so real that I didn't even want him alone with her for any reason. This fear began to consume me. I knew that the only way to move forward with my life was to forgive her for what she had done. I told God that I didn't FEEL like forgiving her. He told me that He knew that but that I must get started in order for the healing to begin. So, as I started to pray, "God, I forgive Grandma for . . ." and as the words were spoken from my mouth, the burden of fear was removed, and the way was paved for me to develop a relationship with my son's grandmother.

Through this ordeal, I came to realize that she was as much of a human being as the rest of us. Most of all, I learned to accept her for who she is and more importantly, to accept her love for me.

Well, we have shared with you the secret weapon of forgiveness that never fails. You are now able to walk in true forgiveness. With this truth of praying for your enemies, you will never be sent back to prison again.

In our next chapters we will give you some tools to help you maintain a life of forgiveness and how to walk it out daily.

CHAPTER TEN
WALKING IT OUT DAILY

It is wonderful to be free. As you have read through this book, you have been able to peel off those layers. It is my prayer that you have come right down to the heart of the matter and dealt with it.

Now that you have paroled yourself from prison, you have been able to taste the good life. Since you now know how bad prison was and how good forgiveness is, it is now time to build a forgiveness maintenance program, one that will keep you continually free. Practice a daily walk of total rehabilitation so that you never return to the broad road of destruction.

In this chapter we will deal with maintaining our relationship with God. This is our greatest asset to obtain our goal. There are three key ingredients that are necessary for intimacy with God: prayer, praise, and the Word.

Prayer is communication with God. Prayer needs to be part of our daily life, as important to us as waking up in the morning. When we talk to someone daily, it is because we have a close relationship with them. We love them and they love us. We want to share everything with them, from our simplest joys to our greatest fears and frustrations.

Daily open communication with God is a sign of a healthy relationship. When we are not communicating with our spouse, our parents, or a friend, it is because of a breach in our relationship. When things are good between us, we enjoy open lines of communication. It is enjoyable to hear what others have to say. God is willing to talk to us about anything and everything. He always has the time to listen to our side of the story.

I have learned if I talk to God about the little things in life, then it is automatic to go to Him when a major situation comes along. If we will talk to God, He will talk to us. Remember, communication is a two-way street. When we have an open line of communication with God, it is easy for Him to guide us. He can talk to us about not getting into a situation that would cause us offense. We can talk to Him about how much it hurt when that person said those wrong things to us. When we talk to God regularly, we have an open line to receive counsel.

Prayer does not have to be in a formal setting. You can talk to God in the shower, the car, at work, the grocery store, or anywhere else you are. You can talk to God like you talk to the best friend you've ever had. He knows all the fancy words, but they are in no way necessary to Him. God loves to hear from you in everyday talk.

Our second key ingredient is praise. Praise, as a way of life, gives you an attitude of gratitude. We all like to be praised, some of us publicly and some of us privately. It is good to hear that we have done a good job and are appreciated. God is the same way. He loves to hear our praises.

God wants to hear our praise for our benefit, not His. God is love. Love does not seek its own. Our praise to Him is to keep us focused on the positive, to keep us upbeat and appreciative. When we thank God regularly for what He has done for us, we stay focused on Him. We are recognizing the One responsible for our success. It keeps us off the path of pride and self-exaltation. Praise works wonders. It gets us out of pity parties real fast.

We all have so much to be thankful for. God has been so good to us. I recall a praise service we had one day. It started out with people coming up thanking God for their job, house, car, the bigger tangible things in life. By the end of the evening, a spirit of humility had permeated that building. We were thanking God for our eyes, our fingernails, being able to walk. So many little things that we take for granted in every day life become important. It was not because we ran out of things to praise God for but that we realized how much we had to praise God for.

> *And we know that all things work together for good to those who love God, to those who are the called according to His purpose.*
>
> Romans 8:28 (NKJ)

We can praise God in all situations, not because God sent them to us, not because we like them, but because all things work together for good. If we will praise God in our tense situation, we have established a trust that will get us through. In the past when an offense came, we would begin to meditate, think, and talk revenge. Now we quickly begin to praise God, realizing that no matter how bad it is, it will only work to our advantage. Praise works wonders. It will keep us off the broad path of destruction.

Our third key ingredient is the Word, giving us a three-bound cord that is not easily broken. The Word, when used on a daily basis, will not only keep us free from the broad path of destruction but also make us successful in every area of life. Joshua 1:8 tells us to be constantly in the Word of God.

> *This Book of the Law shall not depart from your mouth, but you shall meditate in it day and night, that you may observe to do according to all that is written in it. For then you will make your way prosperous, and then you will have good success.*
>
> Joshua 1:8 (NKJ)

We are to meditate on the Word, which means to ponder the Word by talking to ourselves day and night. The only way you can think on something day and night is if you are constantly feeding on it. I know about now many of you are saying, "I could never do that; I can't think on one thing all day."

Well, that's not true at all. Let's look at a couple of ways that many have done this. One example reminds us of what we think on when we become angry and unforgiving. We go through the whole day dwelling on the offense. We would go to bed with it on our mind, dream about it while we are sleeping, and wake up thinking about it. Some of us have done this day after day, week after week, year after year. We were steady and consistent to think on it, wrong as it was.

Another terrific example is when you fell in love. All you could think about was your beloved. You would look forward to the next time you could see them, and if it was not within hours, you would call them. Oh yes, we meditated day and night on that one we loved, longing for the next opportunity to be with them.

As you well know, those relationships that you meditated on day and night did not always make your way prosperous or bring you good success. Thinking continually on the Word always brings good success. Keep in mind that when you were thinking on either love or hate, you still kept your job and continued all your other responsibilities.

Yes, you can do it if you allow yourself to get consumed by it and stay consumed by it. It is easier to obtain something than to maintain it. Getting started and staying with it is the important thing. That is what will bring about great success in our life. It is fun to prosper and be successful, especially if we will do it God's way.

All we have to do is get started reading the Word. Staying in forgiveness gives us the liberty to face the Word daily. The more we read it, the more we will want to read it. Before long it will be an everyday part of our life, something we are not willing to live without. As we see the great results it produces, we only long for more.

Here is a simple program to help you get started reading the Word regularly. There are thirty-one Proverbs, one for each day of the month. Look at today's date, and you will have your Proverb for the day. Proverbs helps us to improve and maintain our relationship with man. You will gain much wisdom as you read and think on these nuggets.

When you're ready, step up to five Psalms a day in addition to the Proverbs. Multiply the day's date by five and that is the last of the five Psalms for the day. For example, on the fifteenth you read Psalms 71 through 75. There are one hundred fifty Psalms, five for each day. These will cause your relationship with God to mature. On the months with thirty-one days, you read Proverbs 31 and Psalm 119.

Psalm 119 is all about how wonderful the Word of God is and lists many of the wonderful benefits we experience from being in the word.

This gets you started. Then you can add some daily New Testament reading, then some Old Testament. Before you know it you are reading the Bible cover to cover each year. It only takes fifteen minutes of reading a day. Who knows, maybe you will read a book of the Bible each day, memorizing whole chapters, and meditating on it day and night. You are well on the road to daily victory.

Praying, praising, and reading the Word all lead to intimacy with God. We cannot be intimate with God and have ought with our brother. With the big three—prayer, praise, and the Word—forgiveness becomes a way of life.

God longs to have fellowship with us for our benefit. He knows that the victory is won in the spirit. We wrestle not against flesh and blood but against principalities, powers, and the rulers of darkness of this age. Forgiveness is a spiritual battle. We need to be in the spirit to win it. This is made possible with an intimate relationship with God.

CHAPTER ELEVEN
SERVING OTHERS

Now that we have learned how to have an intimate walk with God, our daily walk of forgiveness is usually disrupted by our relationships with people. In this chapter we are going to shore up our people skills and look at what will help us in dealing with the offender. Don't think they are going to go away now that you are right with God.

The truth is, you may well have an increase in the number of troublesome folks who try to take you off the path. The enemy wants to get you off the narrow path and back onto the broad one. He knows it leads to prison, and that is where you do him the most good.

In Matthew 23:11-12, we are told that he who is greatest among you shall be your servant and whoever exalts himself will be humbled, and he who humbles himself will be exalted. Servants do not concern themselves with any injustices done to them. Servants look to those in charge and do their bidding. If a beverage is spilled on them, they do not take offense and make a big deal out of their clothes being ruined. They get the proper tools and clean up the mess then continue about their business. When we have the attitude of a servant, we are not offended because we were not invited to a party. We continue on, tending to our duties.

We truly do become great when we are serving others. Serving frees us to be where we are needed, not being where we think we should be. It takes away jealousy, envy, and strife. It eliminates harmful competition that destroys relationships. It puts us in a position to flow, not having to demand our own way.

Let's look at the story of the centurion.

"For I also am a man under authority, having soldiers under me. And I say to this one, 'Go,' and he goes; and to another, 'Come,' and he comes; and to my servant, 'Do this,' and he does it."

When Jesus heard it, He marveled, and said to those who followed, "Assuredly, I say to you, I have not found such great faith, not even in Israel!"

Matthew 8:9-10 (NKJ)

The centurion states that he is a man under authority. A man who is under authority has learned to serve, to put the needs of the one he is serving above his own. This brought him to a position of great faith, greater than Jesus had seen in all of Israel. When you are a servant, you can stay under authority.

Because all authority comes from God, He uses our authorities to get us in the right place. While in the right place, doing the right thing, with the right attitude, we are able to accomplish great things. When we are under authority, our position gives us great faith, a life void of offense. Our heart does not condemn us, and we are able to easily believe. Isn't it wonderful to be a servant and have the joy of faith and freedom from offense?

Being a servant makes it easy to walk in love. The

second greatest commandment, "You shall love your neighbor as yourself," makes it easy to walk in forgiveness. We all want to be forgiven.

One day my daughter helped me to understand "loving my neighbor" in a unique way. My daughter had observed a visiting speaker on a number of occasions in the setting of our own home church. He was always so easy-going and fun to be with. He was never disturbed or overly excited about any of the problems that came up from time to time in our services.

We were attending a conference in this man's church. In this setting he was responsible for the people. When there were mistakes, he took it on personally. As long as it was going on at our church, he had great compassion. He had been through it himself at his own church and could easily understand what we were going through. At his church, however, it was much easier to get upset, to try to solve the problem, and to make things right. At our church he was a servant walking in love, flowing in great under-standing. At his own church, because he was responsible for the meeting, he was always serving but not always walking in the attitude of a servant.

I went away from that session with my daughter realizing that too many times I had taken on cares, stopped walking in love, and not treated others like I wanted to be treated. I came back to our church with a new attitude of love, as one who wanted only to serve, as a teacher who was there to give. It became much easier to handle a micro-phone not working or something being out of order. It is now easier to have compassion, to flow with the situation, to relax and enjoy the moment. I used to get upset when things did not go right. Now I relax, folks understand, and all turns out well.

If we will walk in love and quit getting uptight over things that will not matter in a hundred years, then we can shun the offense and continue to walk on the narrow path of victory.

Since we are serving in love, it is time to start doing kind acts, having a lifestyle of continually doing things for others, not just the routine things we are required to do but out-of-the-ordinary, thoughtful things. When we are living like this, it creates an atmosphere of joy and life.

When we go to the grocery store, we can pick up a cart and take it in with us. Check with a neighbor or a friend before you go to the store to see if there is anything you could pick up for them. Sit down and write a letter expressing your gratitude for a kindness done to you.

Do something that will be a great blessing to someone whom you are not required to help. Pick your wife up some flowers just because it's Thursday. Spend time with the children. Take them to the park, and give them your full attention.

Even though you get to church early, park in the back of the lot and save that close spot for someone else. Help a co-worker who is overloaded by working an hour or two to help them with their job. Cut your neighbor's grass when he is working overtime. Call your friend and tell them you will watch their children if they want to go shopping. Call your parents and say, "I love you, thanks for your invest-ment into my life."

The list goes on and on of things we could do to be kind to those we know as well as those we don't know. The Bible tells us to be kind to one another. One act of kindness can turn someone's day into a pleasant experience.

It's not as much what we do for others but what serving others does for us. Helping others keeps us focused on giving and not taking. When you start being kind, it rapidly spreads to every area of your life. Serving is contagious. It inspires other people and makes us pleasant to be around. We don't have time to dwell on how we have been offended. We are thinking good thoughts and looking for ways to give ourselves away. This keeps us free to let the creative juices flow. We feel better physically, mentally, and spiritually. You will end up getting a better night's sleep. You will wake up refreshed, excited about the day, and looking for ways that you can give to others.

Last of all, in dealing with others, we need to be sure to keep short accounts. Be sure not to let things stack up. Do not let the sun go down before you have made things right. Unfortunately, if we are not wise, things build up quickly and get away from us. We are great for building mole hills into mountains. This blocks our blessings, stops our forward progress, and sets us behind. Too often we look at things wrongly and build a case against ourselves. We want to blame others when all along it was us. Here's Jim's story:

> Not long ago, a brother in the Lord asked me if I would come over to his house and do some work for him. Since I am a plumber by trade, it only made sense that he would ask me to come and do his plumbing. After looking at my schedule and discussing with my wife when would be a good time, I contacted this brother. I told him when I was available, and at that time I also told him how much it would cost.
>
> Well, he was happy with the time frame but was not very happy with the price. Although the price was

less than a third of market value, he felt that I owed him something because of other circumstances. Feeling strange about the situation, I agreed to do the job even though it was for less money.

At first, I wouldn't admit it, but I took an offense. This series of events threw me into a tailspin. I no longer could get any extra work, and my whole attitude in every area of life changed. I felt that I needed to watch every move and make sure I, and everybody around me, was "covered" before doing a job. Looking back, I didn't know why at the time I was becoming more miserable every day. I could no longer hear from God as I usually do on what to charge people or if I should do the job for free. It was horrible. I had never experienced that feeling before. It seemed that anything that had to do with money I couldn't hear from Heaven at all.

After my friend brought to my attention that my attitude about life had slipped to the negative, I immediately realized that I had taken an offense. Unfortunately, it's not always easy to admit on the inside that you are in the wrong. After I admitted I was in the wrong and forgave myself, I immediately was able to hear from God on every job that came my way. I had the renewed freedom because I was not wrapped up in bondage to some offense I took. You see, it was not my brother's fault. I am the one who took the offense. Then I chose to feel that he wronged me when I had agreed to everything from the start. I'm grateful I can view this whole situation as a lesson learned and move on totally free.

We see here that it was because of Jim's own doing that he was having trouble. No one forced him into the job. Had he kept short accounts, he would have avoided a lot of heartache and had more money too.

Take time daily to be sure you have settled all accounts. At the first sign of offense, stop what you are doing and take care of the situation. Remember, you are not responsible for another man's debt. Do what you can do to make it right. Take care of one hundred percent of your part, no matter how big or small that part is. When you go to bed at night, be confident that you have done all you could do to be at peace with all men.

CHAPTER TWELVE
THE KEY PLAYER

Now that we have intimacy with God and right relationships with the people in our lives, we have only one area to work on to round out our daily walk of forgiveness. That area is the parole officer, the main determiner of our course, that's right—it's us. Individually, we decide our own daily walk of forgiveness. We are the key player, the determining factor for success or failure, win or lose, forgiveness or unforgiveness. The choice is ours.

The bottom line is us. We can be taught, encouraged, or reprimanded, and it's our choice that makes the difference. Only one person can be in the batter's box for each pitch. There is no one standing behind you swinging at the pitch if it gets by you.

Sometimes it seems so logical to blame the other guy. After all, it was all his fault anyway. If he had not done that to me, I would not have to react this way. It sounds good, but there is no way to pass the buck. How I am going to respond to what you have done is up to me. Will I take the offense or let it go?

In each situation we are one thought away from either bondage or freedom. The thought we take hold of at the time of the infraction is the most crucial of all. Only we get to select the thought that is taken. Even as a man thinks, so is he. Will you force yourself to think the right thought or allow yourself the pampering pleasure of the wrong thought? Your choice will determine the course of your life. Choose you this day whom you shall serve—freedom or bondage.

We do not truly have freedom to choose until we can make the right choice. People say they do what they want. They choose what they will do. When we make the wrong choice, it demonstrates our inability to make the right choice. When I used to drink alcohol, I proclaimed that I had a choice whether or not to drink. Somehow I would end up drinking. Now that I am free, truly free to choose, I choose not to drink. Before it was not a choice. Before, to drink was a must. Now, I would not have one drink of beer for a million dollars. That is true freedom to choose. I am able to make the right choice no matter what the consequences. It is you who makes the choice when you are free, not the devil, your spouse, or anyone else.

In Luke 17:1 Jesus said to his disciples, "It is impossible that no offenses should come . . ." This is very clear. Opportunities for offense must come and will come. We are all given chances to take an offense. They come to us all, no exceptions. We need to be sure and gird up our loins to protect ourselves from the onslaught. We must hold steady to our commitment to refuse all offenses, no matter what or who the offender is.

Is it worth losing our peace over an offense? Are we willing to pay the price that receiving an offense costs? I pray not. Who wants to be on the broad path of unforgiveness, which always leads to prison?

Yes, offenses will come, but we are going to take an opportunity to pray right now, making a commitment to never again receive an offense. To insure your freedom, pray this out loud:

> Father, I thank You for opening my eyes to the devastation of receiving offenses. I now know that the choice is entirely up to me and me only. I make a commitment today, right now, to receive the grace to never again accept any offense, large or small, that comes my way. I am free from all offenses, and I insist on staying that way. May I continue to be reminded to walk in Your ways. Amen.

To stay away from offenses it is important that we do not judge. Matthew 7:1 says, "Judge not, that ye be not judged." This is a key verse for all of us, one that is short, easy to memorize, and important for us to meditate on. Remember that when we judge someone, it is because we are guilty of the same thing.

Judging is a great big warning bell going off to show us that we have taken an offense. Anytime we see ourselves judging another, we need to stop immediately and start an inspection tour. Somewhere an offense has come in. We need to begin praying immediately for the one we are judging, allowing God to open our eyes to the offense that we have received. Here is Curt's story:

> Over the eight years of my marriage I have taken a few offenses against my wife. Each time I have there has been a frustration inside of me that I can't shake off. I find I am no longer in control of my situation. There is no outward sign of offense in my actions toward my wife, but there is always something inside of me that causes me to be on the defensive.

God has always been able to get my attention and show me areas in my life where I have basically done the same thing my wife was doing wrong and that it was causing me to be in judgment of her. By seeing what was on the inside of me, I was able to turn that offense into compassion and minister to my wife in that area. I did not minister to her by harping, complaining, or quoting the Word but by inward change and action on my part. I was then able to operate in love and expect nothing in return. It was love that provided the power to turn the situation around successfully each and every time.

Another big warning bell is when we need to keep bringing up the same old situation over and over. If the problem is really settled, why does it keep coming up? It's because that old situation is eating a hole in us, which causes it to keep falling out. We cover the hole, and another one eats through. This keeps happening until we finally deal with the situation.

Another big warning bell is when a person walks into the room or you hear his or her name mentioned and you get that sick feeling inside. It is time to start praying for that person and use your secret weapon. God will answer your prayer, open your eyes, and set you free.

I want to close this book with Shirley's story:

To forgive and forget, that is the question! Fortunately, for those of us who claim Christ as our Lord and Savior it isn't a question at all. It is a way of life, and we suffer dire consequences when we make the choice not to forgive.

My very beginnings were probably rooted in unforgiveness. It was passed on to me by my forefathers and mothers! I was born in the '60s to an interracial family and never really had anyone else to identify with and certainly didn't know I was actually created by God. Subsequently, I had many years of questioning my own value and worth along with many jeers and unkind remarks by my peers. My parents divorced when I was nine years old, which added to the load I thought I had to carry.

I began very early on to seek out male attention. I understand now that I was looking for the love of a father. Many times my dad would say he was coming to pick us up for time together. And most of the time my brother and I would sit for hours only to have him not show up or arrive late. Life with mother also proved interesting, as she was left to be both mother and father to two multiracial children. I still remember the strange looks we would get at the mall—a white woman with two Afro-American kids. I still don't think she ever figured out how to manage my nappy hair.

My search for my father's love led me along a path too lengthy to mention. Needless to say, I looked for love in all the wrong places and I have had to forgive not only the men who took advantage of that quest but also myself.

My forgiveness process has been slow and steady. I would stress that for me it has been a process, not like taking a pill to instantly dispel the pain.

Through Christ's love I now realize my parents did the very best they could at raising me, and I am grateful for that. My father has come to know the Lord. What right do I have, after all God has forgiven me for, to hold anything against him. He now has a great relationship with my family and me. We have begun to restore the ground unforgiveness stole from us all. Both of my parents have been a great source of God's love to and for me.

This process doesn't come easy for me, and I often want to issue only partial forgiveness. However, a little doesn't go a long way. I learned this the hard way.

Eight years ago, I discovered my husband had a fling while I was out of town. My trip had been framed in deceit, and I reaped deceit when I returned, but that is another story! Upon learning of his indiscretion I was faced with a choice. I heard God say it was time to break the curse of divorce and it was to begin with me. I chose to forgive my husband, or so I thought.

For the next eight years I lived in agony caused by the bitterness I had sunk into. Three years after the affair I discovered a lump in my breast. I truly believe it was a result of my bitterness. As a result, I opened the door to breast cancer. My treatment and cure would take too much time to tell about. The good news is I am now cancer free and intend to stay that way! My love and faith in God and my husband were tested during this time, but both proved faithful to me in ways I cannot even express.

This part of the process came to a crashing halt in August, eight years later. I discovered a note from my husband to a girl he worked with. I stormed to his job and burned up our car's engine in the process. When I confronted him with the note, my husband assured me the note was as far as it went. He had been convicted by God and threw the note in the trash (that is where I found it). He had no involvement with this girl, and she never knew that he was interested.

Well, I didn't believe him and was convinced this junk had started again. I spent the next 30 days in the pits of hell being tormented with my bitterness. Unfortunately, everyone around me and everything I touched was contaminated by my bitterness. I was the victim again and out of control.

I had an appointment with a counselor and was convinced they would side with me. I knew they would read my husband the riot act. Boy, was I wrong!

After hearing the facts, they looked at me with great compassion and said to me, "You never forgave him the first time. You must forgive him to go on." I realized I needed to do that. You see, my unforgiveness eight years ago had contaminated my heart and thoughts, and consequently my words and actions. I spoke disrespectfully and angrily about my husband. Is it any wonder we were having problems?

I left the counselor's office in total disarray. I cried out to God and asked for help. God assured me that this was true and that He would be there with plenty of grace to help me forgive totally and completely.

I had to pick my husband up from work that night, and I met him with those gut-wrenching sobs we all know. Imagine his surprise and relief when I asked him for forgiveness for my deception and unforgiveness. We both cried together that day. My entire life and marriage turned around. I genuinely love my husband and family as well as those around me. Our love life has radically changed. We now walk in unity and are receiving all God has for us.

I'm grateful God didn't let up on me. I'm also thankful for my pastor who shared the truth of forgiveness with me. My life would be hell if I had stayed where I was.

Shirley's story is a powerful one. It places the focus on the key player—ourself. The price is too high to pay for unforgiveness. The years of misery are too costly for us and the ones we love.

It is up to me; it is up to you. There is no buck to pass. Forgiveness is a one-man show, and we are the star.

God will abundantly bless you as you walk on and maintain the path of forgiveness.